PORTFOLIO / PENGUIN

DREAM YEAR

Ben Arment runs Dream Year, a coaching organization that helps turn dreams into reality. He also runs an annual conference for thousands of creators, dreamers, and entrepreneurs called STORY. He lives with his family in Virginia Beach, Virginia.

www.dreamyear.net

DREAM
YEAR

Make the Leap from a
Job You Hate
to a Life You Love

Ben Arment

PORTFOLIO / PENGUIN

PORTFOLIO / PENGUIN
An imprint of Penguin Random House LLC
375 Hudson Street
New York, New York 10014
penguin.com

First published in the United States of America by Portfolio / Penguin 2014
This paperback edition published 2015

.
ISBN 978-1-59184-729-8 (hc.)
ISBN 978-1-59184-794-6 (pbk.)

Printed in the United States of America
1 3 5 7 9 10 8 6 4 2

Set in Sabon
Designed by Pauline Neuwirth

To Ainsley

CONTENTS

DREAM
YEAR

INTRODUCTION

Never let the odds keep you from pursuing what you
know in your heart you were meant to do.

—SATCHEL PAIGE

You Were Born for This

After this year, I want everyone to look at your life and say, "Ahhh, but of course." I want them to hear the faint sound of a proverbial "click" as your experience, gifts, passions, and platform all converge into one beautiful endeavor.

When this happens—when you are finally doing what you were born to do—it won't feel like work. Don't get me wrong—there will be sweat on your brow; you'll be overwhelmed at times; and there will be moments when you feel like giving up. But it will be welcomed hardship.

There are two kinds of work. The first kind contributes to someone else's vision and gain. Most people are doing this kind of work, which is why country music songs about five o'clock whistles and happy hour are so popular. This kind of work comes with intolerable bosses, slow-moving time clocks, and closely scrutinized paychecks to make sure the bookkeeper got it right.

The second kind of work contributes to your own life's purpose. Sure it's difficult, but the reason behind it makes it easier to get out of bed in the morning. You don't tell anyone this, but you'd do it for free. It's the occupational equivalent of a "runner's high" where you've broken through the side cramps and short-windedness, and now you're beaming as the landscape moves rapidly past you.

Some people are content to do the first kind of work and help fulfill the dreams of their employers. But my guess is you're not one of them. You were born with a dream of your own. And this year, you're doing something about it.

By reading this book, you are moving toward a new kind of work. This year, we are going to discover a viable, profitable, and sustainable "idea model" that brings your dream to life.

This is your dream year.

1

DARING TO DREAM

A ship in harbor is safe, but that is not what ships are built for.
—JOHN A. SHEDD

Frustration Shapes a Dream

As you enter this next year, I'm counting on one thing from you—that you're frustrated. If you were to say, "No, I'm doing great. Everything's fine. I just want to try out this new idea," I'd be worried. If you weren't discontented, heartsick, or angry about something in the world, you would have no reason to go after your dream.

Without frustration, you'd never even recognize your dream, let alone have the courage to pursue it. Going after a dream is hard. And frustration is the fuel that propels you through the challenges when your idealism runs out. There are going to be times when you'll need that frustration. You'll need a "worse time" to help you get through the difficult times ahead. Frustration is the grit that motivates you to pursue your vision. It makes you unwilling to go back to the way things were before you decided to act.

When people get frustrated, most of them respond by complaining. And you can't blame them. Bad bosses, no money, workplace injustices, terrible customer service, the lack of an affordable option—we've all been there.

But we can also respond to frustration by dreaming. We can take the same agonizing circumstances and use them to create a fresh, new vision for the future. To do this, you and I must learn to see frustration as a gift.

After all, frustration shapes a dream.

There is something missing, something lacking, or something unjust happening in the world, and the only one who seems to notice it is you. But that's how it's supposed to work. You notice a problem that no one else is addressing, and it eats at you until you're finally willing to do something about it.

Who knew frustration could be a good thing?

In 2010, Ben Nockels of Oklahoma City experienced a frustration that he could not shake. He learned that there are 408,000 children in the foster care system in the United States. He also learned that out of this population of abandoned kids, more than 107,000 are adoptable. In other words, their parents' rights have been terminated or relinquished. In Ben's words, these kids "are never going home." They have no sense of place, no sense of belonging, and are not part of any family.

For the kids who are not placed in foster homes, there is only one outcome—they'll remain in the system and languish until they age out at eighteen. And history shows that those who age out of the system don't fare well in society. They'll face incarceration, addiction, joblessness, and even premature death.

Overwhelmed by this frustration, Ben joined my Dream Year coaching program to figure out a solution. He started with his home state of Oklahoma. As of January 1, 2012, there were 8,308 children who were in the custody of the state. Ben met with the leaders of the Oklahoma Department of Human Services and learned that 1,500 additional families were needed to place kids in homes. Ben believed the best place to find those families was the faith community.

So Ben launched the 111 Project, which mobilizes congregations to place foster kids in the homes of loving families. The "111" stands for one church, one family, and one purpose. Ben figured out that there are 6,100 churches in the state of Oklahoma. So if every church committed "one family for one purpose," they would leave no Oklahoma child without a home. This was Ben's dream.

So far, hundreds of families have joined Ben's effort.

Make History

When you're frustrated, you can choose to complain about it, run from it, or ignore it. But if you decide to do something about it, you'll make history. This is the gift your dream brings to the world.

What great dream is frustration birthing in you?

When Fred Astaire and Michael Jackson were both alive, they shared an unlikely friendship. Although their dance styles were completely different and their musical tastes worlds apart, they shared a strong connection out of the public eye. When a reporter asked Fred Astaire about their unusual relationship, he surprised everyone by admitting that they both danced out of anger.

Now, we have reason to believe that Michael Jackson did. His dance style was aggressive, and he often decried the loss of his childhood. But who would have guessed that the graceful and elegant Fred Astaire was motivated by anger? It was a deep-seated, well-hidden motivation, but what a gift it turned out to be.

The scariest moment is always just before you start.

—STEPHEN KING

Our unfortunate circumstances can become the impetus for something great. But first we have to learn how to turn our frustration into a vision of something good. Those tragic experiences don't have to be wasted on you. You don't have to become reactive and withdrawn or let bitterness render you useless. You can birth a fresh new dream for the future that redeems your life and benefits other people as well. As you'll discover, that's what those experiences were meant for all along.

When Howard Schultz acquired Starbucks and launched what would eventually become the number-one coffee brand in the world, he allowed one of his greatest frustrations to shape the company's unique culture.

When Howard was a small child, he came home from school one day to find his father, an uneducated blue-collar worker, lying on the couch with a broken hip and ankle from slipping on a patch of ice at work. Without any health insurance or workman's compensation, he fell into poverty and depression.

Remembering his father's struggle, Howard vowed that he would never let it happen to his own employees. He acknowledged that his father's experience shaped his company's employment policies and benefits. To this day, Starbucks offers its "partners" generous health benefits and stock in the company. No wonder Starbucks has been able to preserve such a strong, people-centric culture. Howard's frustration fueled his passion.

Whenever we complain about our circumstances, it's usually because we think someone else should do something about it—someone more talented, more gifted, more influential, and more authoritative. But eventually, when no one else steps up to the challenge, we realize the vision belongs to us. It's frightening. It's intimidating. But once we've suffered through enough frustration—it's inevitable—we simply must do something about it.

The Antidote to a Bad Job

On a recent business trip across the country, I visited several friends who work at various companies. On all of these stops, each friend pulled me aside to express frustration with their jobs. The complaints included bad work conditions, abusive bosses, pay reductions, unnecessary rules, limited freedom, and negative coworkers.

It's not that I'm unsympathetic, but I don't believe there's a bad job that a great dream can't fix.

Most of us have jobs because someone constructed a financial model that utilizes our skills for their own gain and pays us just enough money to make employing us worthwhile to them. Someone else gets to be the boss. Someone else gets to determine our pay raises and work hours. Someone else gets to create the work culture and call the shots.

I'm here to tell you that nothing is stopping you from constructing your own system to sustain your livelihood. You can create a model that offers value to other people in exchange for money. You don't have to depend on other people's dreams. You can bring your own dream to life. The work isn't easy. You'll be stretched beyond what you think you can handle. But there is nothing more satisfying than getting paid to pursue your own dream.

Once in a while it really hits people that they don't have to experience the world in the way they have been told to.

—ALAN KEIGHTLEY

We have entered the entrepreneurial age. It's not so much a new era as it is a return to a society of independent "makers." But instead of producing wooden tables, horseshoes, and handmade hats, this new generation of makers is developing Web sites, offering consulting services, writing books, launching brands, and offering accounting services from a home office or coworking space.

In their book *The Start-up of You*, Reid Hoffman and Ben Casnocha argue that we can no longer expect to *find* a job, but rather we must *make* our own jobs. Thomas Fisher, the dean of the College of Design at the University of Minnesota, wrote that our generation of entrepreneurs, either because of intention or layoffs, will grow to 40 or 45 percent of the workforce by 2020 and become the majority by 2030.

Studies show that 66 percent of Americans hate their jobs. They despise their bosses, bemoan their working conditions, and feel like they're not making a difference in the world. On top of this, they're frustrated by a dream that's never been realized. In a recent survey, UPS found that 48 percent of Americans dream of starting a small business.

And it's not just because people are becoming more entrepreneurial. It's because there aren't enough jobs to go around. According to Gallup polls, 3 billion people in the world say they want to work, but there are only 1.2 billion full-time, formal jobs. In other words, there are 1.8 billion more people than jobs in the world. In the United States, the Bureau of Labor Statistics reports that 12.7 million people remain unemployed, while only 3.5 million job openings exist.

Many college graduates are no longer bothering to apply for jobs but opting to start their own businesses, preferring to keep their occupational fate in their own hands. In 2009, Arizona State University students Mehdi Farsi, Reza Farsi, and Eric Ferguson forsook conventional jobs and started the State Bicycle Co., which makes fixed-gear bikes called "fixies." In just four years, they opened three stores and employed twenty-five people.

Even our homes will begin to reflect the needs of a "maker" society. In 2012, Clemson University students Eric Laine and Suzanne Steelman won the international Dow Solar Design to Zero competition by designing a house for the entrepreneurial age that features commercial space on the ground floor and living space upstairs.

You can do this.

You probably won't launch a successful idea on the first attempt. You might fall on your face a few times. You may have to adjust the model, change the formula, and tweak the concept until it finally works. But if you learn from your mistakes, get better at what you do, and refuse to quit, you will accomplish your dream.

You're a Good Horse

At the 2009 Kentucky Derby, eighteen Thoroughbreds ripped out of the starting gate and pounded into the straightaway. The pack mostly stayed together until the first turn, when the field started thinning out. Spectators kept their eyes on the favorites as the announcer recited their names over the loudspeaker. But suddenly, at the third turn, an overlooked horse at fifty-to-one odds burst into the lead from the inside.

Mine That Bird had a long-standing losing streak. He wasn't a contender to win, not by a long shot. So when he emerged at the front of the pack, the announcer stumbled over his notes to find his name. As Mine That Bird blasted across the finish line far ahead of the other horses, the announcer could hardly contain his surprise: "A spectacular finish! A spectacular finish!"

He declared the victory to be "an impossible result."

When the jockey, Calvin Borel, was asked how Mine That Bird could have possibly won, he said, "I rode him like a good horse."

Imagine that.

He instilled faith in his horse to win.

He believed in him.

Dream Year is founded on the basis that most of us get ridden like bad horses all of our lives. Perhaps we had parents who put us down; friends who made fun of us; bosses who insulted us; or colleagues who underestimated what we could do.

Even worse, we fell for it.

I remember when a boss told me "You're not good enough" after I volunteered to lead a project at work. Another boss mockingly referred to my journal as my "happy book" because I was constantly writing down ideas—some of which you are reading now. I remember all of those incidents as if they were yesterday, and some of them crippled my courage. They caused me to doubt myself.

We need jockeys who believe in us, who treat us "like a good horse."

If Mine That Bird could come from behind to win the Kentucky Derby, you can benefit from the faith of other people as well.

Have you heard of those studies that show how children perform in school at the level of their teachers' belief in them? It's true. You are the product of the voices in your life. And it's up to you to decide who to listen to.

You're a good horse. Surround yourself with people who believe in you. If you've got naysayers in your life, ditch the stall they put you in and find another jockey. Go achieve an impossible result.

Your Only Gatekeeper Is Courage

All of us have dreams we want to bring to life. But, like glorified beggars, we hold them out like empty cups, waiting for someone else to fund them, approve them, or give us an opportunity. There was a day when gatekeepers determined whether your project got launched.

You got discovered.

You got funded.

You got green-lit.

You got picked up.

You got approved.

This has always been the conventional pathway. But not anymore. The best way to get your project launched is for *you* to launch your project.

Today, your only gatekeeper is courage.

We are no longer living in the Industrial Age when you needed large amounts of capital to fund your ideas. You don't need a publishing company to print your book. You don't need a Hollywood studio to make your movie. And you don't need a venture capitalist to fund your start-up. All of the tools, funding, approval, and distribution are already at your disposal.

You are about to embark on a journey to discover how to monetize your dream. You probably have no idea how you'll fund it yet. But this is the challenge of every dream chaser. We'll explore some financial models, try a few experiments, and find the path to making your dream sustainable.

Several years ago, my friend Larry sent me a screenplay for a sitcom he had written. We talked about next steps, wondering how he could get it into the hands of someone in the industry. The chances of someone in Hollywood reading his script were slim. So what of his dream? Did he have no shot?

I happened to know the general manager of a television studio that is located in my friend's very own town. I called him and learned that the studio—with cameras, lighting, and dressing rooms—sits vacant for much of the week. The general manager said he'd be glad to give my friend a tour of the studio and schedule some test shoots. My friend only needed to recruit some actors and build a set.

That same week, I read an article in *Fast Company* that described how homemade sitcoms are sweeping the industry. The president of FX Networks, John Landgraf, insists on producing comedies such as *It's Always Sunny in Philadelphia* and *Wilfred* with small budgets. I also learned that actor Edward Burns has been making movies, such as *Newlyweds,* on consumer-grade cameras with small crews, short time lines, and budgets of just $9,000. Apparently, low-budget films and television shows that perform well are what the industry is looking for.

My friend didn't have to offer up his dreams to the whims of gatekeepers. He only had to muster the courage to bring his own dream to life. The resources were all around him.

And that's exactly what he did.

Larry enlisted some friends to build a set, create costumes, and volunteer their talents in acting and videography. He's preparing to shoot the first episode of a sitcom called "Cousin Bigfoot" about a Sasquatch that comes to live with an ordinary suburban family, claiming to be their distant cousin.

There's no telling whether Larry's sitcom will catch on and get picked up by a studio. But he decided to give himself permission rather than wait for someone else.

> **People who say it cannot be done should not interrupt those who are doing it.**
>
> **—GEORGE BERNARD SHAW**

In 2010, Kate Schmidgall from Washington, D.C., joined Dream Year to start her own magazine called *Bittersweet.* Her dream was to create an artistic, documentary-style magazine that profiled organizations doing inspiring and much-needed work in response to the critical social issues of our day.

Convention says that Kate should have held out her dream to other magazine publishers or investors, asking them to fund her publication. With the rising costs of paper, printing, and distribution, there's no chance they would have said yes. But Kate was determined to find a way to publish it herself.

She used profits from her design business to print the first few issues, and then got creative to find more funding until the advertising and subscription dollars kicked in.

With a passion for helping developing-world entrepreneurs overcome their difficult circumstances and start businesses, Kate started buying their products at fair-trade prices and selling them in her magazine for a profit. Her solution was to create a publication that was half magazine, half catalog. The sales of the products not only benefited the makers, but also helped fund the magazine.

It requires no courage to come up with an idea and wait for someone else to green-light it. You're asking the *gatekeepers* to have courage. You're asking *investors* to accept the risk. You're asking *someone else* to have faith in your dream.

But what about you? Do you believe in your idea enough to bypass the conventional gatekeepers and bring it to life on your own? It might mean finding sponsors, crowd-funding your idea, applying for grants, bartering services, freelancing, asking friends for help, or even working a part-time job. But there is a way. There is always a way. You only need the courage to go after it.

You, as it turns out, are the only gatekeeper for your dream.

Becoming Comfortable with Risk

You are about to enter a season of risk. You're going to invest resources, time, and hard work to bring a dream to life. It's going to feel like you're risking everything.

Make no mistake about it—your dream is not safe.

But what is safety? Your so-called safety rests in the hands of a volatile stock market, a moody boss, a fickle economy, the latest real estate appraisal, and stable health. You have no control over any of it. The safety you imagine for yourself is merely a matter of perception.

This isn't to say you should quit your job right now. Pursuing a dream isn't about being irresponsible. It's about designing a system—just as your boss did—to give value to other people for a price that sustains your livelihood and grows the business.

The other day, a friend told me he lost his job.

"All this time," he said, "I thought I was playing it safe by working for my company. But if there's no security there either, I might as well pursue my dream."

Risk doesn't feel very good. It's agonizing, actually. But you can acclimatize. You can adjust to it. Adventurers who climb Mount Everest have to arrive at least one week early to get used to the altitude. But their bodies adjust.

You can adjust to the climate of risk as well.

In an interview with ESPN, Malcolm Gladwell talked about how people in high-stress jobs learn to function with the pressure. He told the story of Gavin de Becker, who runs one of the top personal security agencies in Los Angeles. He provides bodyguards for celebrities, dignitaries, and moguls.

De Becker described the process he uses to train his employees. He said that if "the quality of our coordination and instinctive reactions breaks down when our heart rate gets above 145," he exposes them to stressful situations over and over again until they can face them at 130, 110, or 90.

"So he fires bullets at people," Gladwell said, "and does these utterly terrifying exercises involving angry pit bulls."

The first few times you go through these exercises, you basically lose control of your bowels. But by the fifth time, your essential bodily functions begin to return. And by the tenth time, you can function like a normal human being.

Throughout the course of this year, you will be challenged, pressed, pushed, and agonized. But that's the way it's supposed to be. When you launch a dream, the size of it should overwhelm you. You should have wind in your hair, stomach acid in your teeth, and pee in your underwear.

But you will get used to it. You will calm down. You will stop freaking out. You will make it through the hardship. And everything will be okay.

You can learn to pursue your audacious dream with all of its risks, fears, and stresses and still function as a normal human being.

The Two Fears

We are motivated by two conflicting fears in life—the fear of failure and the fear of insignificance. What we endeavor to do in life is determined by which fear is the strongest.

Throughout my life, I have gone back and forth between the two fears, as I've forgotten what it's like on the other side. I've been terrified at the prospect of losing my life savings. And I've been frightened at toiling my whole life away on other people's dreams. But I've made my choice. I have decided which one I will fear the most. I want to do something significant with my life.

I choose the fear of insignificance.

You must choose which fear will be the strongest for you. If you don't choose one of them, one will be chosen for you. And it will be the fear of failure, each and every time.

I talk to many people who aren't doing what they love but hold on to their job because it pays the bills. They don't pursue a dream because it feels irresponsible or even irrational. After all, a job allows them to provide for their families, buy things they enjoy, and put away savings for the future. But if you press on with these excuses, the underlying motivation is fear.

> **By acting as if I was not afraid, I gradually ceased to be afraid.**
> **—THEODORE ROOSEVELT**

We only need to cite a worst-case scenario or a close brush with disaster, and we're done dreaming. We can't fathom the prospect of being jobless, not paying our bills, or having a financial emergency. It doesn't matter that worst-case scenarios rarely happen. And even when they do, they're not as bad as we think. We can survive them.

In fact, what most of us call a worst-case scenario is often just a reduction in our standard of living. We can't imagine being without cable TV or a second car.

As we grow older, dreams don't disappear. We trade them in for standards of living.

Look, if it becomes as bad as you'd feared you can always get another job. You can recover your life savings. You can get your dignity back. But you can never recover what you never tried at all.

Choose the Fear of Insignificance

On February 18, 2012, *The New York Times* printed the obituary of a man who was unknown to most people. He never wrote a book. He never started a company. He didn't even have his own Web site. But at seventy-four years old, John Fairfax died at his home in Henderson, Nevada, having seized every opportunity that life afforded him.

Here are a few of the highlights:

- At nine years old, he settled a fight in the Italian Boy Scouts with a pistol.
- At thirteen years old, he became a trapper in the Amazon jungle.
- He studied literature and philosophy at a university in Buenos Aires.
- At twenty, distraught by a broken heart, he let a jaguar attack him in the jungle but ended up killing it anyway.
- He joined the crew of a pirate ship in Panama, mastered the skill of navigating the high seas, and became the captain of his own boat.
- He managed a mink farm and worked as a professional gambler.
- He crossed both the Atlantic and the Pacific oceans by rowboat, was attacked by a shark, and killed another one by outsmarting it.

Reading through this list, you might think John Fairfax was a superhero, a legend, or a cartoon character. But he was simply a man who refused to let his life be tamed by the cubicle. He didn't base his decisions on a paycheck, the fears that haunted him, or the expectations of people around him. He saw the world as an adventure, something to be exhausted, and he lived it to the fullest. He was the original "most interesting man in the world."

Your dream may not be to kill a shark with your bare hands, but there is something great rising up in you. People may have tried to squash it. You may have failed at previous attempts. Or maybe your dreams have simply given way to comfortable standards of living.

This book is about getting them back.

You were born to live a significant life.

Call to Action

Your dream lies at a crossroads of your fears and frustrations. While others may see these emotions as annoyances, for the dreamer, they are the indicators of vision. They not only show you what's important to you; they provide the fuel to sustain your passion through the difficult seasons of dream chasing.

The first step in daring to dream is figuring out what frustrates you. Remember that what you complain about is what you're gifted at. What bothers you the most is usually the area of your greatest passion. So complain. List your gripes. Identify the injustices and absences that frustrate you the most. And then be prepared to do something about them. You could wait for someone else to do it. But they won't. Your burden is your mandate. This is the very reason you were born.

The second step is to determine what frightens you most about pursuing your dream. There are only two options—the fear of failure or the fear of insignificance. Make the choice to face your fear of failure and make this your dream year.

QUESTIONS:

1. Your dream is not safe. Don't apologize for being reluctant to pursue it. But what frustrations are burning inside of you that could help dampen these fears?
2. You'll come to see that frustrations are a gift because they birth our dreams. What possible solutions could come out of your frustrations?
3. If you don't choose a fear, one will be chosen for you. Are you more afraid of pursuing your dream than not pursuing your dream? If so, how can you cultivate a healthy fear of insignificance?

DEFINING THE DREAM

The two most important days in life are the day you are born and the day you discover the reason why.

—MARK TWAIN

Your Great Gift

There is no such thing as a "dream job."

Jobs aren't designed to bring your dreams to life. They're designed to bring *other* people's dreams to life—those of the founder, the owner, the CEO, or the boss. The point of Dream Year is to bring *your* dream to life.

The trouble is you've been trained for a job your whole life. You've been conditioned to believe that your personal value is based on what you can do for someone else. No one ever asks you what *you* can bring to the world but whether you can fill a position.

Think about the job interview. It's about trying to convince someone that your square peg of talents fits into their round hole of a position. It's you against all of the other square pegs vying for the same slot. You can only hope you're the closest fit.

One of the remarkable outcomes of pursuing your dream is discovering what *you* were born to do—your great gift. It's not to be a cog in someone else's machine but to align *what you do* with *who you are*. When you figure this out, you'll find more satisfaction and make a bigger contribution to the world than any job could provide.

You are a unique individual with distinct passions, experiences, and skills. Of course no perfect job exists for what you can do. You've only just come along in the world. You have to create this role for yourself.

Have you been waiting for permission to do this?

Permission to do what you love.

Permission to work on your own ideas.

Permission to determine your own income.

Permission to pursue your own dream.

If no one else has granted permission to you, let me be the first to say—you are allowed to do this. You can stop trying to fit into someone else's mold.

If you're unsure of your dream, know that you're already pursuing it in some form. It may be a hobby or a fascination with a particular field. Or it may be the thing you admired in others before you forsook it to pursue a more "reasonable" career. But the clues are all around you. This year, we're going to uncover them one by one until you are able to articulate a clear, definitive dream for your life.

Your Dream Has a History

Your dream existed long before you were aware of it. Perhaps you've spent years bouncing from idea to idea until you finally discovered the real one. But it was always there waiting for you. If you look back over the experiences of your life, I'll bet you can see traces of it.

If you're an entrepreneur, you'll see hints of risk taking all the way back to your childhood. If you're an artist, you'll remember the joy of making projects that graced your family's refrigerator. If you're an activist, you'll remember caring about social injustices and wondering why no one else did. All of us have "defining moments" that forecast our dreams and helped shape our potential.

Carl Bass majored in mathematics in college and spent his early career working as a software engineer, all while pursuing his great love for craftsmanship in his own woodworking shop at home. Now, as the CEO of Autodesk, he has the perfect history for leading a company that specializes in 3D design, engineering, and builder-based design software such as AutoCAD, SketchBook, and Pixlr. It's the culmination of all of his talents and passions.

All of our dreams have a history.

As an event producer, I've created numerous conferences, concerts, and festivals and have consulted on dozens more. When I look back over my personal history, I can identify numerous defining moments that led me into producing events. When I was a kid, the children's minister at my church was a Barnum & Bailey–trained circus clown who inspired me with events that were nothing short of spectacular. In college, I worked backstage at rock concerts, which helped me understand concert production.

While working at my first job as an advertising copywriter in Dayton, Ohio, I organized a summertime concert series that would attract teenagers who had nothing better to do on Friday nights than grope one another in the local Kmart parking lot. A few years later, I organized my first conference, called the Whiteboard Sessions, which was a grassroots success, drawing nearly one thousand paying attendees. This led to working for a large leadership conference before I finally mustered enough courage to launch STORY, my own conference for creators, dreamers, and storytellers, in Chicago.

All of these defining moments served as trail markers for my own true calling. I never sought out these experiences. They guided me. To this day, I love nothing more than producing live events. The truth is, I never really had a choice.

Career expert Penelope Trunk once wrote: "Do you want to know what you should do right now? Do you want to know what your best bet is for your next career? Look at what you were doing when you were a kid. Nothing changes when you grow up except that you get clouded vision from thinking about what you SHOULD do—to be rich, or successful, or to please your parents or peers—the possibilities for 'should' are endless."

Realize that your dream is not about starting something new. It's about rediscovering a great passion that was abandoned in favor of societal expectations, false security, ill-conceived motives, or more comfortable standards of living.

Too many of us are not living our dreams because we are living our fears.

—LES BROWN

The movie director Guillermo del Toro, whose films include *Hellboy* and *Pan's Labyrinth,* didn't just stumble into making horror films. It was the product of his life's fascination with all things grotesque and morbid.

When he was a young boy in Guadalajara, Mexico, he frittered away his afternoons by dissolving slugs with table salt in the city sewers. He owned a stuffed werewolf and begged his mother, a tarot card reader, for a mandrake root that he could use for black magic.

At a grocery store, he discovered a magazine called *Famous Monsters in Filmland,* which showed him how to simulate flesh wounds and human deformities using home-baked materials such as gelatin and collodion.

As a teenager, Guillermo came across a man with a split skull on the street and helped him get to the hospital, only to end up volunteering for the clinic. One day on the job, he came across a waist-high pile of fetuses in the embalming department, which he says upended his Catholic faith and turned him into an atheist.

Among the other atrocities he witnessed were a decapitated teenage boy who had driven into a barbed-wire fence on his ATV; a driver who had caught on fire and couldn't get out of his truck; and his own father's kidnapping, which lasted seventy-two days.

Stripped of his innocence, Guillermo occupied himself by making movies about monsters. He went on to attend film school and start his own special-effects company for low-budget movies that needed frightening creatures.

In 1993, Guillermo arrived in Hollywood at a time when the film industry's monsters were less than realistic. His aim was to make them more lifelike, more authentic, and more terrifying. He would often sacrifice his own salary in order to increase the film's budget for special effects. It led to making films such as *Mimic*, *The Devil's Backbone*, and *Mama*.

Guillermo, it seems, had no choice but to make monsters for a living. Every experience, every fascination, and every terrifying incident from his past led him to one inevitable conclusion. You can see his time line practically shape his dream.

Your Past Shapes You

If you were to create a time line of your dream, what would be on it? Can you look back and see traces of your passion? How about relevant experiences?

Your dream has a history. And knowing where it showed up at various moments in your life will give you the confidence to pursue it.

Ask yourself these questions:

1. In what areas have I excelled?
2. What were the defining moments of my life?
3. What passions or interests can I *not* shake?
4. What are my frustrations?
5. What hard work would I gladly do for free?
6. What kinds of people are drawn to me?
7. What comes easily for me?
8. Where do my gifts collide with what other people want?
9. What were my interests and tendencies as a child?

After living all this time, accumulating experiences, improving your skills, and growing your passions, why would you ever abandon this personal history to start something new? Your dream is the outcome of a life lived up until this point, not a new beginning. You don't go after your dream. Your dream comes after you.

In 2012, a Dallas attorney named Thomas Boto joined Dream Year to fulfill his dream of creating an animated children's book series. As the father of two little boys, he wanted to read them bedtime stories that showed the beauty of nature and taught them faith-based values.

After some initial brainstorming, he came up with the idea for "Owlegories"—a classroom of owls who travel the world and learn lessons on their adventures.

Thomas initially hired an artist to design the characters, but the samples looked computer generated and impersonal. After months of unsuccessful revisions, Thomas finally sent me a few sketches that stood apart. The new characters were rudimentary yet adorable, simple but compelling.

I urged Thomas to tell me who drew them.

"Do you like them?" he asked.

"I love them! Who did it?"

"I did," he said.

Who knew that Thomas the attorney was also a talented children's book illustrator? When I asked Thomas whether he'd ever aspired to be an artist, he said, "I loved to draw when I was younger and all throughout school. I even drew a cartoon for the cover of our high school yearbook."

Thomas told me that his grandmother was a gifted artist and calligrapher. She hung paintings throughout her home, along with her brother's artwork, whose pieces hang in the Smithsonian American Art Museum.

Thomas said, "Thinking back, some of my favorite school memories came from class projects that required creativity. One of my all-time favorite classes was in eighth grade, when we got to use the old Disney animation software and create our own five-minute animation. I created a story about a snail that saves the world."

Thomas clearly has a history to his dream.

Your dream has a time line. And it didn't start just now. You have been shaped and prepared for it by the experiences of your past. Your dream has been holding out for you, waiting for the right moment to reveal itself. You don't have to strain to come up with a dream for your life. It's been waiting for you all along.

Tragedy or Trajectory

Not one single experience has been wasted on you. What you might have thought was a worthless endeavor, a big mistake, or a pointless job was exactly what you needed to experience for what's ahead.

In an interview with James Lipton on *Inside the Actors Studio*, the legendary film director Steven Spielberg said that his father, who was a computer scientist, and his mother, a musician, got divorced when he was a young boy. It had such a negative impact on his life that he admitted the movie *Close Encounters of the Third Kind* was his way of trying to get a computer scientist to communicate through music.

Colin Meloy, the lead singer and songwriter for the Portland-based band the Decemberists, once described the unique sound of their best-selling album *The King Is Dead* this way: "When my parents got divorced, my dad took the Stones records and my mom took the Neil Young records, so I guess this record is my way of getting the albums back together."

There is no experience, no broken relationship, no childhood memory, no horrible job, and no tragedy that is wasted on you. It all culminates in one beautiful composition of experience, motivation, and purpose. This is the way great dreams are born into the world.

You can view the bad things in your life as either tragedy or trajectory. It all leads to something magnificent.

What if heartbreak and setback were qualifications for your dream? What if your dream required thick skin and you didn't have it? Would you be okay with facing heartache after heartache if it helped prepare you?

What if before you could be used greatly, you had to be wounded deeply? Would you be willing to exchange pain for greatness?

Artificial Dreams

All throughout college, I wanted to be a writer, so I majored in English, interned at a newspaper, and then worked as a copywriter at an advertising agency until I finally got sick of it. It was too much work for too little reward.

You could say I wasted years on trying to launch a writing career, but it prepared me for my real dream. It gave me the tools to pursue my true calling. Writing has been the foundation for every project I've undertaken.

Every experience you have either steers you away from the wrong dream or contributes to the real one. When you have this understanding, you can face the death of your artificial dreams with a sense of anticipation for what's to come. Your life is being equipped with exactly the kind of experiences your true dream requires.

Richard Branson never set out to be a business tycoon. But the failure of his first venture—a magazine called *Student*—forced him to move in a different direction. "I wanted to be an editor or a journalist," he said. "I wasn't really interested in being an entrepreneur. But I soon found I had to become an entrepreneur in order to keep the magazine going."

When you suffer a setback, rest assured that it's making you better. When your finances are tight, know that you're developing survival skills. When you are dismissed or misunderstood by your industry, know that you're growing as a visionary. When you're fined or penalized, know that you're being educated about important legal requirements. No matter what failures befall you, be confident that you're one step closer to breakthrough.

You could easily become discouraged when you look back on all of the broken dreams in your life. But I encourage you to look more closely. You'll see a beautiful tapestry of experiences that helped shape you into the dreamer you are today. You are better not just because of your successes but also because of your failures.

The Dream That Only You Can See

Don't be surprised if other people don't fully embrace your dream or even understand it right away. Skepticism and doubt are welcomed barriers that keep other people from doing what you do. When they fail to understand what you're doing, consider it a gift. You have a dream that only you can see.

One day, people will come to embrace what you see. But until then, consider your isolation a safe laboratory to work out the kinks in your dream, to try and fail without the scrutiny of others.

It's kind of fun to do the impossible.

—WALT DISNEY

When Sergey Brin launched Google with cofounder Larry Page, they took advantage of their obscurity by improving the site before more people used it.

"We knew that Google was going to get better every single day as we worked on it," Sergey said. "So our feeling was that the later you tried it, the better it was for us because we'd make a better impression with better technology. So we were never in a big hurry to get you to use it today. Tomorrow would be better."

When others haven't been visited by your frustrations, when they haven't been blessed by your dreams, they can't imagine a better solution. The reward of being a dreamer is that you get to create an unseen future. Henry Ford reportedly said, "If I had asked people what they wanted, they would have said faster horses."

The downside is that you may suffer criticism, even ridicule.

Walt Disney had a difficult time persuading other people to believe in his dreams. He had to pay for movie productions and theme park drawings with his own money until his business partners finally saw the vision too.

On the opening day of Walt Disney World in Orlando, a man

commented to the television host Art Linkletter, "It's too bad Walt didn't live to see this."

"But he did," Art replied. "That's why it's here."

What you're doing might seem impossible to other people, but it shouldn't stop you from doing it anyway.

You've been given the gift of obscurity, of doubt, of impossibility. Relish the opportunity to make history with your dream. One day, other people will see it too. As Nelson Mandela said, "It always seems impossible until it's done."

THEY SAID IT COULDN'T BE DONE

If your dream doesn't make sense to others, don't lose heart. You're in good company. Here's what was said about some of the greatest dreamers in history:

"We don't like their sound, and guitar music is on the way out."

Decca Recording Company, rejecting the Beatles, 1962

•

"Heavier-than-air flying machines are impossible."

Lord Kelvin, President, The Independent Scientific Academy of the UK, 1895

•

"Wasting her time. She's too shy to put her best foot forward."

The drama school that dismissed Lucille Ball

•

"The telephone has too many shortcomings to be seriously considered as a means of communication."

Western Union internal memo, 1876

•

"There is a world market for maybe five computers."

Thomas Watson, chairman of IBM, 1943

•

"He is too stupid to learn anything. He should go into a field where he might succeed by the virtue of his pleasant personality."

Thomas Edison's teacher

•

"Lacked imagination and had no original ideas."

The reason a newspaper editor gave for firing Walt Disney

•

"Who the hell wants to hear actors talk?"

Harry Warner, founder of Warner Bros. Studios, 1927

•

"You ain't goin' nowhere, son. You ought to go back to drivin' a truck."

Jim Denny, the manager of the Grand Ole Opry, to Elvis Presley in 1954

Your Sweet Spot

When we come upon people who are working in their sweet spot, we tend to think it was their ideas that made them successful. But we fail to recognize all of the necessary ingredients that went into their life's work.

Amazon isn't a business that just anyone could have started. Jeff Bezos was conditioned his whole life to launch the top e-commerce site in the world.

As a toddler, Jeff showed a remarkable aptitude for mechanics when he tried to dismantle his crib. As a teenager, he revealed his entrepreneurial tendencies by quitting a job at McDonald's to start an educational camp for children called The DREAM Institute. He charged $600 and prescribed a reading list that included his favorite books—*The Lord of the Rings, Dune, Gulliver's Travels,* and *Treasure Island.*

After pursuing a career in science, Jeff worked for a Web start-up that taught him *what not to do.* Then he left for Wall Street to work in the area of technology. It was at this hedge-fund job that he realized how Internet-based shopping could converge with his passion for books, technology, and start-ups. Amazon was born out of this scenario. No one else could have seen this coming. It was the perfect storm of experience, skill, opportunity, and passion.

Discovering your dream is about finding your sweet spot. It's where these four components—passion, demand, platform, and giftedness—come together in one coordinated expression. A dream isn't something you just make up for yourself. It's what life has been preparing you for all along. Maybe you don't see it yet. Maybe your artificial dreams have kept you looking in other places. But when you finally see how these four components come together into one perfect expression, it will all make sense. You'll recognize your dream. And you'll want to do nothing else.

Passion

Bringing your dream to life requires tremendous passion to withstand the challenges that come with it. Without passion, you become distracted by every excuse, opportunity, and diversion. Think of all the successful bands that stopped making albums, the famous actors who stopped making movies, and the best-selling authors who stopped writing books. It's a shame when great dreamers run out of steam.

Demand

Ideas are worthless when there's no demand for them. Services fail, causes flop, and products flounder when people don't want them.

For your dream to take off, it must meet a need, solve a problem, or satisfy a craving. Sometimes you can get lucky and stumble into demand on the first try. But most times, you discover it with trial and error. You have to fall on your face a few times before you finally figure out what people want.

Platform

You can have a great idea and the passion to deliver it, but without a ready-made audience, you're sunk. Mark Ollila, the director of media at Nokia, once said, "If content is king, distribution is King Kong," When you have a platform, such as a Twitter following, a mailing list, an online community, or an event, you can go straight to your audience. Without a platform, you either become a glorified beggar, asking other people to share it with the world, or you have to pay for advertising.

Giftedness

An idea is only as good as the person who creates it. A project is only as strong as its weakest part. If you're making a film, bad acting will sabotage beautiful cinematography. Poor writing will destroy a good book. And bad singing will end a musical career. But keep in mind: your giftedness can have one of two expressions.

The Producer or the Artist

You can come at your dream as the "artist" or the "producer." When I refer to the "artist," I don't mean someone who paints, sculpts, or sketches. It can be, but I'm talking about the craftsman— the person who delivers the offering. It could be the writing, the number crunching, the coordinating, the designing, the performing, or even the leading. But the producer recruits the artist to do the actual work.

The producer is the visionary who brings a project to life through other people. They may not be great at the craft itself or they may be brilliant at it, but they know how to direct the efforts of other people in a masterful way. The producer orchestrates the project to ensure its success. The dreamer becomes the coach.

Ed Cash was a talented singer and songwriter who traveled the country performing for students at youth camps. If anyone was going to succeed in music, it was Ed. He had a great voice and a strong gift for songwriting. But his big break never happened. He never got signed to a label or caught on as an artist. But singing wasn't the only way to express his gifts. He started producing other people's albums.

Ed now lives in Nashville, writing best-selling songs and shaping the sounds you love in other successful artists. In fact, he was named Producer of the Year for four consecutive years at the Gospel Music Awards.

Too many people stop short of their dreams because they believe that being the "artist" is the only way to carry out their craft. But it isn't. They can also be the "producer" for other "artists" to carry out the same vision.

We've been trained to come at the world as artists, to do it all on our own. But what if we're not supposed to? Someone who is not a doctor can own a medical practice. A white-collar businessman can start a blue-collar construction company. And a nonathlete can own, manage, or coach a sports team.

This might challenge how you think about your dream. But what if you entrusted the work of your dream to someone else? You'd still have control. You'd still make the decisions. But you wouldn't necessarily be the one to do the work. In fact, becoming the producer might be the very thing that helps your dream succeed.

As Malcolm Gladwell explains, mediocre players can make great coaches, just as great players can make lousy coaches:

"Top athletes so often make bad coaches or general managers. They often don't really know why they were as good as they were. They can't describe it, which means that they can't teach it and they quickly become frustrated at their inability to lift others up to their own level. Mediocre players—or nonathletes—tend to make better coaches because their knowledge isn't unconscious. It's the same thing with writing. I know very little about science. But I think I write about science more clearly than many scientists, because I have to go over every step, carefully and deliberately."

If your dream requires the talent of other artists, take pride in becoming the curator, the editor, or the director. You'll join the ranks of amazing producers like Guy Laliberté, the creator of Cirque du Soleil; Anna Wintour, the editor of *Vogue*; Scott Belsky, founder of the Behance Network; James Cameron, the director of *Titanic* and *Avatar*; and Chris Anderson, the curator of TED.

These visionaries might be brilliant artists in their own right, but their greatest gift to the world comes from coordinating the efforts of other talented people.

How to Beat Learning Curves

You know you're facing a learning curve when the very thought of pursuing it makes you breathe heavier. You're afraid to confess your inaptitude to other people, so you cite other excuses, like not having the time or the interest. Maybe you'll do it next year when things calm down.

But without scaling learning curves, you'll stay the exact same person next year that you are this year. And the next year. And the year after that. Before you know it, you're one of those people at the high school reunion who has nothing to show for the time away. You didn't become the best version of yourself.

Dreams come a couple sizes too big so you can grow into them.

—REVEREND RUN

For years, I've wanted to write and produce a feature-length film. Writing is not hard for me. I've been a short story writer, an advertising copywriter, a newspaper reporter, a magazine columnist, a blogger, and an author. I write at least four thousand words every week. But the thought of writing a screenplay has always felt daunting to me.

Screenplays have their own format and structure. I've never been able to make sense of the Courier typeface, the three-act structure, the cryptic abbreviations from scene to scene, and words like "logline." Until now.

In my fight up the learning curve, I read every book on the subject of screenwriting I could get my hands on. I ordered original screenplays to study and rented classic movies so I could analyze their structures. At first, I reread chapters over and over until I finally understood the terminology. I nearly gave up on several occasions.

But then I broke through a wall.

Now I can tell you the "inciting incident" of any movie I've watched, not to mention the plot points, where act 1 breaks into act 2, the midpoint, and so on.

There's no shortcut to learning new things. You have to submit yourself to the humiliation of asking questions, the hardship of understanding difficult concepts, and the time commitment to practicing the craft. But there is no level of comfort from the status quo that beats the feeling of accomplishment.

Here's how to beat learning curves:

1. You buy the staple books of that industry and read them.
2. If you hate reading, you take a class or go to a workshop.
3. If you didn't understand what you read, you read it again.
4. Put the books away and start practicing the craft. A lot.
5. Reach out to people ahead of you and ask questions.
6. Go to the places of your industry, as awkward as it may be.
7. Find a mentor.
8. Start putting out the work, even if it's not perfect.
9. Keep putting out the work, each one better than the one before.
10. Wake up one day to find that you're standing on top of the curve.
11. Then look for the next one.

THESE THINGS WEREN'T MYSTERIES ANYMORE

When Steve Jobs was in elementary school, his next-door neighbor, an engineer at Hewlett-Packard, introduced him to Heathkits, which were electronic do-it-yourself kits. He started building radios, amplifiers, and battery testers in his own garage.

He said, "These things were not mysteries anymore."

Uncovering the mystery of electronics is what gave Steve the insight to create a revolutionary computer company.

Steve said, "The kits gave a tremendous level of self-confidence that through exploration and learning one could understand seemingly very complex things."

Mystery paralyzes us. It makes us feel like we can only do what we know. This is why tinkering is so important. Experimentation is the antidote to mystery.

Demystify Your Dream

I've always loved how David Copperfield transports his audience to another world through magic. He wraps his illusions in mysteries. He doesn't just make someone disappear. He lures us into a grand mystery that manipulates our emotions. For example, he'll tell the story of a haunted house that has claimed the lives of numerous victims over the years. Then he'll invite an audience member on-stage to experience it. The music will pulsate, the lights will dim, and David's voice will become serious and suspenseful. By the time the person disappears, we actually believe the haunted house is real.

But the mystery of David Copperfield's illusions came crashing down for me when my wife Ainsley and I attended one of his shows a few years ago. Shortly after taking our seats, my wife felt a tap on her shoulder by an assistant who wanted to know if she'd like to appear in an illusion. "Of course!" I exclaimed, practically pushing her out of her seat. They took her backstage, where they explained how the illusion was going to work, and then brought her back before the theater filled up.

At the appointed time in the show, Ainsley was "randomly selected" from the audience to go up onstage, where David switched her underwear with those from another "random" female volunteer while "Thong Song" blasted in the background. As her husband I probably should have been appalled by the spectacle, but as a David Copperfield fan, I have to admit I loved it.

As my wife explained the trick to me, the mystery of the illusion was shattered in my mind. So were David's other tricks. I began researching how he walked through the Great Wall of China, how he made the Statue of Liberty disappear, and how he made ghosts fly above the heads of the audience. I peeked behind David Copperfield's curtain, and it's not as impressive as you might think.

I'm telling you this because many of our dreams are shrouded in mysteries that keep us from achieving them. We glorify authors, mystify filmmakers, and lionize thought leaders, which makes their success seem unobtainable. We're in awe of our dreams, so we hold our work up to these impossible standards that keep us from pursuing them.

In reality, the activities of our dreams can be broken down into a series of steps that are more mechanical than mysterious. We become so enraptured by the mystery of David Copperfield walking through the Great Wall of China that we fail to see that he was rolled away in a secret compartment in the staircase.

Our dreams consist of mechanical activities that wouldn't impress anyone. How books get written, how films get made, how businesses get started—the necessary work is much less impressive than the final result.

Robbie Coltrane, the Brittish actor who played Hagrid in the Harry Potter movies, was once asked how the filmmakers made him appear so large on-screen. He refused to answer on the grounds that it would ruin the magic of the movie.

There is a dream conspiracy at work. What we think took enormous amounts of unattainable talent actually came from hard work.

What mysteries are keeping you from doing the unimpressive work of your dream? Are you so enamored with the idea of being a public speaker that you pursue the fruit of the labor, rather than the labor itself? Building a platform is the product of a lot of hard work, not merely talent and passion. Are you skipping the unimpressive parts for what you see onstage?

Is it the mystery of launching a business? Most people think that successful businesses are the result of an epiphany. But businesses succeed because of years of trial and error. Their founders learn what to do by discovering what *not* to do.

Frans Johansson, the author of *The Medici Effect*, said, "Everyone we regard as brilliant has endured an enormous amount of failure."

Great business ideas come about because of course corrections and failed experiments. Frans went on to say that the biggest difference between effective innovators and ineffective ones is the quantity of ideas. That's quantity, not quality. Successful innovators simply generate more ideas.

Or is it the mystery of being an author? Is your dream to be a published author who has an agent, collects big advances, and garners prestigious speaking gigs? That's fine, but don't neglect the unimpressive work that's required to get you there. No one can do the difficult work of your dream but you. You'll have to pound out every single one of those seventy thousand words on your own.

One of the greatest authors of our generation, Cormac McCarthy, who wrote *The Road*, *All the Pretty Horses*, and *No Country for Old Men*, once described the outright poverty he endured throughout his career as a writer. He wrote more than five million words on a secondhand typewriter that he bought for $50 from a pawnshop in Knoxville, Tennessee, in 1963. Yet most of us only look at how that same typewriter sold for $254,500 at a Christie's auction in 2009.

You can be inspired by the mysteries of great dreams. But to achieve them, you must pull back the curtain and do the unimpressive work that gets you there.

Solve a Problem

Before you take one step toward your dream, answer this question: What problem are you trying to solve?

It doesn't have to be a matter of social justice or charity. It could be the lack of a good restaurant in your city, a rarely addressed subject in books, or the absence of a particular kind of mobile app.

If there's not a problem, if there's not something lacking that your dream is going to provide, why should anyone care about what you're doing?

At the Willow Creek Association's 2010 Global Leadership Summit, Bill Hybels talked about the importance of calling people from "here" to "there." He said that leaders often focus on the wrong side. They tell people how great it's going to be "there" without pointing out how bad it is "here."

People need to see a problem to be moved.

Whoever best describes the problem is the one most likely to solve it.

— DAN ROAM

According to screenwriting experts, one of the components of a great film is an "inciting incident" that occurs early in the story's plot. It presents a great problem that confronts the main character and sets the story in motion. For Harrison Ford in *The Fugitive*, it was being accused of his wife's murder. For Mel Gibson in *The Patriot*, it was the murder of his son by a villainous British officer. The inciting incident propels us into the story and keeps us on the edge of our seats until the problem is solved.

Let me ask you a question. What was *your* inciting incident? What was the problem that incited your dream and introduced a great hope into your life? Is it a problem for other people as well?

It's a beautiful thing when your dream collides with the needs of other people. In fact, it's the only way for your dream to succeed.

Dan and Chip Heath once described the difference between marketing aspirin and vitamins: "Vitamins are nice; they're healthy. But aspirin cures your pain; it's not a nice-to-have, it's a must-have."

It's better if your dream is like aspirin. You don't want to spend all of your time trying to persuade people to embrace something they don't think they need. You want to cure their headaches. You want them to crave what you have to offer.

So how can you frame your dream as the solution to a problem?

When Chuck Templeton created the restaurant reservation service OpenTable in 1998, he discovered that restaurateurs didn't need it or want it. Danny Meyer, the owner of Union Square Café, told him, "Look, I don't need more business. We're full every night." There was no problem.

That could have been the end of Chuck's business. But rather than giving up, he reframed his dream to offer restaurants a "guest management" platform where they could access detailed customer data. This is something no restaurant had access to but many desperately wanted. Chuck didn't change his core offering—it was the same management system—but he reframed the way he presented it to meet a need. OpenTable now serves more than thirty thousand restaurants throughout the world.

When your dream offers the solution to a problem, the world awakens to your idea. People return your phone calls; they say yes to your proposals; they volunteer their time; they subscribe to your mailings; and they line up to buy your products. Your dream sells itself because it addresses a great need.

What is the great problem your dream solves? If it doesn't solve a problem, how can you reframe it so that it does?

Name Your Dream

People often ask me: "What if I don't know what my dream is?" But in most cases, they already do. They're just too afraid to say it. Voicing a dream makes it real. It's terrifying and delightful all at the same time. It means that with any good conscience, they have to do something about it.

This awareness motivates some people to act and causes others to cower. Naming a dream invites tough decisions. It may require taking a risk, leaving a job, or dealing with insecurities. Naming a dream unsettles our comfortable lives because we can no longer spend our free time lounging around while the hard work of the dream is waiting for us. And who goes looking for discomfort?

Naming a dream fills our heads with doubts, fears, anxieties, and insecurities. We ask the question—*who am I to think I can do this?* We feel small compared with this great calling we've been avoiding all of our lives. Every dream has a dark side. The minute we start pursuing it, the burden becomes bigger than the idea.

Author Steven Pressfield describes the phenomenon of pursuing "shadow careers" that look similar to our real dreams but entail no risk. It's the aspiring filmmaker who settles for making corporate videos. It's the aspiring novelist who pursues a Ph.D. in literary studies instead. It's the entrepreneur who goes caroming from one job to the next, hoping that each new start will satisfy his urges.

We can be brilliant at creating excuses for not pursuing a dream. But this year, it ends. This is your Dream Year. Name it. Identify it. Call it out for what it is.

Naming a dream is a powerful catalyst because it holds us accountable to our calling—both from our supporters and our critics. Peer pressure can be devastating in junior high school and gated communities. But when it comes to your dream, social pressure can be one of the most helpful forces on the planet.

I won't mince words. Pursuing a dream is difficult. It requires things of you that have never been called on before. It changes who you are and leaves you never the same. I don't know about you, but I don't want to be the same person in five years that I am today. I want to be the best version of myself.

Every cycle of Dream Year produces a similar pattern:

Month 1—You're terrified but excited about actually having to
    do this.
Month 2—You're intimidated and wonder if this was a mistake.

Month 3—You strain to adapt your idea to a more effective
  model.
Month 4—You're overwhelmed and want to take a break or
  quit.
Month 5—You begin to see your dream take shape through
  branding.
Month 6—You make some "big asks" that surprisingly pay off.
Month 7—You adjust your idea to suit people's needs.
Month 8—You start acting less like an employee and more like a
  CEO.
Month 9—You use "we" instead of "I" as a team forms around
  you.
Month 10—You're tempted to stop asking questions and settle
  for where you've landed, but you must fight this tendency.
Month 11—You begin to see revenue coming in from your
  efforts.
Month 12—The dream is no longer in your head. It's an
  organization with a working model. There's a plan for
  growth and sustainability.

You can do this. But it starts with having the courage to name your
dream. At first, you'll be frightened by the prospect of pursuing it.
But it will be worth it. And not just for you. This is for everyone it
inspires, for the loved ones around you and for those who come into
contact with your great gift to the world.

Call to Action

You don't go after your dream. It comes after you. Your dream is
the culmination of all the experiences, gifts, passions, and opportunities you've ever had in your life. It all amounts to a unique expression that only you are capable of bringing to the world. The first
step in determing your dream is to write out your personal history
in the form of a time line. List all of the experiences that were significant in your life. They could be good or bad, wonderful or tragic.

But identify the experiences that left an indelible mark on your life. For these hold the clues to what your dream could be.

Nothing is ever wasted on you—no tragedy, no setback, no failure, and no diversion. After you write down your personal time line, can you see where your true dream emerged? Can you see the times when you deviated by pursuing an artificial dream? Are you pursuing an artificial dream now? It might be frightening to get back on course. You may have to mourn the loss of a fruitless ambition. But the sooner you can get back to your true dream, the better your life will be.

Be honest about what you're gifted to do and what you're not. Just because you're not gifted to be the practitioner of your craft doesn't mean you can't pursue it. But you may have to recruit other "artists" to do the work of your dream. This isn't a demotion. By becoming the "producer" you'll join the ranks of talented people who orchestrate the efforts of others—magazine editors, film directors, music producers, conference organizers, and CEOs.

Now name your dream. Take a whole month to wrestle with it if needed. But don't go any further in this book until you can name it.

QUESTIONS:

1. What is the history of your dream? List the defining moments in your life, for better or worse, that shaped a dream within you.
2. What are some artificial dreams you've pursued? How did these setbacks and misguided ambitions prepare you for your true dream?
3. What problem does your dream seek to resolve? If it doesn't address a problem, how can you reframe it in such a way that it does?

3

YOUR IDEA MODEL

**If you're looking where everybody else is looking,
you're looking in the wrong spot.**
....
—MARK CUBAN

It's About More Than an Idea

So you have an idea. Everyone has an idea. And what's worse is a lot
of people have *your* idea. We have entered an age in which great
ideas abound. Everyone has something they're trying to promote.
It's no longer novel to have just an idea.

What you need is a new idea model.

An idea model takes a concept and turns it on its head. It changes
how people engage with the idea and challenges the practices of its
industry. It creates an idea that is not only uncommon but also more
compelling.

When you buy a pair of TOMS shoes, you're not just buying one
pair of shoes for yourself; you're giving another pair to someone in
need. When you buy a ticket to Cirque du Soleil, you're not just going to the circus; you're paying for a theatrical experience. These
organizations created new idea models.

Most people's ideas are rather conventional. They dream of a retail store, a book, a nonprofit organization, a design firm, a social
justice campaign, a speaking career, and so on. But to be effective in

a crowded marketplace, you have to create a new idea model. You have to reinvent the industry.

In 1999, Robin Chase and her husband lived in Cambridge, Massachusetts, with just one car to share between them. Robin drove it so infrequently that she couldn't justify buying a second car, but she would have loved to rent one for a few hours here and there. With the Internet taking off and the use of cell phones rising, Robin figured a car sharing service would go over well in a place like Boston.

So in 2000, she raised money from friends, recruited her husband to be the chief technology officer, and launched Zipcar by positioning four cars throughout the city, renting them by the hour. Each car was outfitted with a card reader that would only grant access to the member who reserved it online. The business spread from Boston to Washington, D.C., to New York and then the rest of the country.

Robin created a new idea model by looking beyond taxicabs, bikes, and buses as the only modes of transportation and introduced a whole new category for commuters. By now, the idea of car sharing is a conventional one. But when Robin started Zipcar, no one would have dared to leave an unattended rental car sitting along the street. She created a radical new model for the industry. And it paid off. In March 2013, Avis purchased Zipcar for $500 million.

Before you go any further with your dream, think about how you can reframe your idea so that it stands apart from everyone else's ideas.

If your idea is a pizza shop, your challenge is not to copy the conventions of the industry. It's to figure out a surprising new twist on pizza shops. Maybe it's made-to-order pizza at your table by a "pizza master." Maybe it's a radical departure from conventional ingredients. Or maybe it's a pizza truck that sells hand-held pizza roll-ups to pedestrians. It takes multiple attempts to find the right model. You won't know what works until you try. But when you finally do, you'll be the first one in your field; competitors won't exist yet; and your industry will never be the same.

There's a danger in loving your first idea too much. As my friend Sarah Bray says, "Most ideas aren't bad. They're just not done." We tend to come up with conventional ideas because they're familiar to us. They feel like safe bets. But the world is full of familiar ideas that drift into obscurity. Conventional ideas are actually riskier. Let's step back from our ideas and evaluate them through a new lens. Our goal is to create an idea model that awakens the world to a new experience.

Break the Rules of Your Industry

The prevailing form of creative inspiration is imitation. We copy what others have done in the past. If we're starting a marketing company, we position ourselves like all of the other marketing companies. If it's a social justice organization, we adopt the same tactics as other causes. We try to look "the part" of our particular industries in a misguided effort to gain respect. We scour the Web, steal from those other guys, borrow strategies from the market leaders, and otherwise perform creative piracy.

But you can't compete this way. You can't stand apart by being the same. You can't break out from the pack by looking like everyone else in your field.

So don't compete.

Break the rules of your industry.

Every good thing that has happened in your life happened because something changed.

—ANDY ANDREWS

Fabien Riggall was a short-film producer in London who noticed a lapse in the kind of experience you could have at film festivals compared with the more popular music festivals. Music festival attendees were more engaged at their events with dancing, drinking, and sing-alongs, whereas film festival attendees just sat there.

So in 2005, Fabien created Future Cinema, an immersive moviegoing experience where audience members became part of the story line. The screenings included theatrical elements, live musical scores, actors, props, and stage sets. "People want to experience culture, not just be given it on a plate," Fabien said.

At a showing of *Grease*, Fabien's team transformed a rented venue into the halls of Rydell High. For months leading up to the event, they collected props such as satin Pink Ladies bomber jackets, pool tables, bad-boy leather jackets, and cheerleading outfits for more than a hundred actors who brought the film's theme to life.

"People are striving for real experiences, whether that's bicycling or supper clubs," Fabien said. "Why I think this works is that people dress up, they feel relaxed, they talk to people they might not have met at a cinema. It's a social experience."

This led Fabien in 2007 to create Secret Cinema, which incorporated the same theatrical elements as Future Cinema but didn't allow moviegoers to know which film they were going to see until they arrived at a secret location. Secret Cinema's tagline warned participants to "tell no one."

At a showing of *Lawrence of Arabia*, attendees were greeted by horsemen in Middle Eastern garb, led across a park, and finally ushered into Alexandra Palace in London, where they encountered a marketplace full of food vendors and live performers. They watched the movie while reclining on cushions and "magic carpets."

In January 2012, Secret Cinema sold nearly nineteen thousand tickets to its longest-running event for the movie *The Third Man*, charging $72 a ticket. Then Hollywood came calling. Fabien was hired to stage an experience for Ridley Scott's *Prometheus*, which drew twenty-five thousand people to thirty sold-out shows. They had more ticket sales than the local IMAX theaters.

In October 2012, Fabien announced he was taking Secret Cinema to New York City and other major European cities. He's been talking to Hollywood studios about staging four to five events a year and building online communities for new movie releases. Even more, he recently launched Secret Restaurant and Secret Hotel to extend the concept of surprise experiences.

To be original requires a new way of looking at your industry. Rather than making lists of inspiration, trolling the Web, or copying the ideas of other people—start with a list of rules. Identify the conventions by which your industry operates. Then ask why those rules exist. And break them.

Here are some rule breakers who disrupted their industries with new idea models:

- Nathan Blecharczyk, Brian Chesky, and Joe Gebbia broke the rules of the hotel industry when they asked why complete strangers couldn't stay in people's spare bedrooms when they traveled. They launched Airbnb in 2008 and, by February 2012, reported more than 5 million nights booked in people's homes.
- Artist Gabrielle Bell broke the rules of portraiture by using the videoconferencing tool Skype to find clients. For just $35, she paints portraits of people from all over the world on 3½-by-2½-inch acid-free cards with black ink and watercolor. People simply log on to their Skype accounts for sittings.
- Scott Morrison broke the rules of manufacturing denim jeans in 2011 by launching a made-to-order studio called Paper Denim & Cloth. Eleven seamstresses produce six thousand pairs a year from a studio in New York City where visits are by appointment only and guests can choose from seventy-five bolts of varying types of denim.
- Stephen Fowler, who owns The Monkey's Paw bookstore in Toronto, reinvented bookselling when he came up with a way to sell his unpopular stock of used books. He created a vending machine called the Biblio-Mat that distributes a surprise book. The sign on the front reads: "Every Book a Surprise. No Two Alike. Collect All 112 Million Titles." He discovered that people value the surprise of an obscure title more than the same book sitting in a bargain bin.
- Ken Johnson and Andrew Draper broke the rules of selling men's underwear in stores by launching Manpacks, which ships undergarments to customers by subscription every three months.
- Five graduate students from New York University broke the

rules of e-mail by creating a project called The Listserve, which sends subscribers one random e-mail a day from a complete stranger. The content includes everything from advice and short stories to personal reflections. More than twenty-four thousand people have signed up for the list since April 16, 2012.

- Will Ramsay in London created the Affordable Art Fair as a way to help fine artists make money by selling their works to ordinary people at street fairs. He's defying the elite art world, which has historically been a closed community, by bringing great art to the masses all over the world.

- Peter Gelb, who manages the Metropolitan Opera, is breaking his industry's status quo by making performances available to the masses with live satellite broadcasts to movie theaters through National CineMedia's digital network. Now people across the country can enjoy live performances, along with those in New York, at their local movie theater.

- Ben Milne from Des Moines broke the rules of the credit card industry by creating Dwolla, which processes payments, but doesn't take a percentage of the cost. He only asks for 25 cents, whether the price is a dollar or a thousand dollars. The company processes more than $350 million in transactions each year.

Now it's your turn. Write down all of the rules and conventions of your industry in every conceivable category and ask, "Why do we do it that way?" or "How can we break that rule?"

THE REINVENTION OF THE VIDEO RENTAL INDUSTRY

Let's look at the rules of the video rental business. This is how most video rental stores such as Blockbuster and Hollywood Video operated in the 1990s:

1. Offer videos for rent in conventional retail storefronts.

2. Display the empty boxes for people to peruse.

3. Charge several dollars for each rental.

4. Require customers to return videos within two days.

5. Charge an additional fee for late returns.

Now let's look at how Netflix broke those rules:

1. Offer videos for rent on a Web site.

2. Use the U.S. Postal Service to deliver and return DVDs.

3. Charge a monthly subscription fee for unlimited rentals.

4. Allow customers to return videos on their own time line with no late fees.

5. Replace lost DVDs for free.

Starting in 2002, a competitor, Redbox, reinvented the rules yet again:

1. Offer videos for rent in kiosks outside of grocery stores.

2. Allow people to reserve DVDs on the Web for pickup.

3. Charge one dollar per day for rentals.

4. Make the total price dependent upon however many days the customer decides to keep the rental.

With the rise of competitors, Netflix moved the industry online:

1. Offer streaming movies online for a cheaper price.

2. Raise the prices on mailed DVDs to encourage Web streaming.

3. Attempt to separate the DVD and streaming business.

Now that companies such as Hulu, Amazon, HBO, and iTunes offer streaming movies as well, the industry is begging for reinvention yet again. Research shows that digital downloads, streaming media, and on-demand sales will increase tenfold by 2017.

Create a Property

I once attended a seminar about the economics of making movies led by Perry Lanaro, the vice president of corporate financial systems at Paramount Pictures. If anyone knows how films become green-lit, it's Perry. He oversees spreadsheets at one of Hollywood's top studios.

One of the attendees asked him about the best way to pitch a movie from a financial perspective. Perry responded with this suggestion: "Don't pitch a movie. Create a property that studios will want to make into a movie."

By "property," Perry wasn't talking about real estate. He was talking about ideas, characters, cartoons, brands, stories, concepts, or art that could be turned into a film. In other words, if we focused on creating great ideas that resonated with people, the movie would take care of itself.

At a Dream Year Weekend in Nashville, a young publishing executive named Nubia Echevarria approached me to talk about her dream. She asked some general questions about manufacturing, distribution, and marketing until my curiosity got the best of me and I implored her to share the idea.

Reluctantly, she reached into her purse and pulled out the most adorable little stuffed monkey you've ever seen. His name was Otis the Love Monkey.

"You made this?" I asked.

Nubia's face beamed as she described her dream. She envisioned a line of stuffed monkeys that would be featured in children's books and videos to teach kids about character qualities. She had enlisted a community of women in Peru to hand-stitch the monkeys in a fair-trade agreement. And the proceeds of book sales would go to various charities that are making a positive difference in the world. Nubia now produces two characters, Otis and Penelope, along with books and T-shirts, under a brand called The Monkey Project. By giving life to such lovable characters, Nubia created a property that can extend across multiple platforms.

Creating a property gives people a better framework to value your offering. Nubia could have just as easily started a charity to raise money for struggling Peruvians. She could have held fundraisers and launched awareness campaigns, but it would have competed against every other conventional charity in the world. Instead, she created a family of sock monkeys that teach character qualities, delight kids, *and* benefit women and children in Peru. As a property, "Otis the Love Monkey" flipped the value proposition. Now everybody wins.

You may not be making movies or inventing characters, but there's an important lesson here. If you focus on creating a strong property, you won't have to work so hard to promote it. Great ideas spread. They can't help themselves.

When the TV series *Mad Men* debuted in 2007, it was devoid of any recognizable stars. The actors were all relatively unknown. So in order to promote the series, AMC's head of marketing, Linda Schupack, determined to "sell the enigma" of the smoky, self-destructive advertising culture of the 1960s. Posters of noir-style admen were plastered all over Grand Central Station, while actors dressed in period costumes handed out business cards from Sterling Cooper, the show's fictitious ad agency. The show's property was its biggest asset. They only needed to amplify it. In 2013, *TV Guide* placed *Mad Men* sixth in its list of the sixty greatest dramas of all time.

Where the Sidewalks Have Been Trodden

The most common downfall of dreamers is holding fast to an idea and being unwilling to change it when it doesn't work. The point is not to be right about your idea but to be effective. One way to be effective is to leverage proven ideas.

There is a legend about a university president who refused to pour the sidewalks in a new expansion of the campus until the students started using it. He argued that when the students trampled down the grass on the pathways they preferred, the sidewalks would reveal themselves. If the university tried to determine these paths in advance, they'd end up with a lot of dead grass and unused concrete.

The same is true of your dream. The right path is waiting to be discovered. But if you make a big investment before it's proven to work, you could get it wrong.

The perfect expression of your dream is waiting to be discovered— the one that resonates with people; the one that satisfies market demand; the one that works. Right now, it's invisible. You can't see it. But it's there. Your job is to look for the natural pathways that people take and then to pour the concrete of your idea.

You can find these invisible paths by looking for what works in other markets. Howard Schultz of Starbucks brought the espresso drinks and sense of community from Italian coffee shops to America because he saw it working so well overseas. Reed Hastings of Netflix brought the monthly payment structure of fitness centers to the video rental industry because it didn't penalize the customer.

Here are some ways to minimize the risk of your ideas:

1. Identify the "Pain Points" of Your Industry

Your idea won't succeed if it doesn't solve people's problems. Ask yourself what "pain point" your dream addresses. Drew Houston asked himself why people kept e-mailing themselves large files to store online. It was faster to store files in e-mails than to save them on external hard drives. So, in 2007, he created an online storage system that people could access from anywhere. The result was Dropbox, which now has 175 million users and more than $200 million in revenue.

2. Start with Small Experiments

I once asked a restaurant mogul how to start a successful ice cream parlor. He suggested opening a temporary pop-up store in the local mall to test flavors and gauge the community's response. This way, you wouldn't lose a large investment if it failed, but you could get a foothold in the community if it succeeded.

3. Only Invest Money You Can Afford to Lose

The point of Dream Year is not to "go for broke." It's to mitigate your risks and make wise investments in the pursuit of your dream. Learn from small attempts. Once you figure out the formula, you can risk more knowing you have a plan that's proven to work.

4. Never Stop Improving the Idea

Once you launch a successful idea, it won't be long before competitors are nipping at your heels and fighting for market share. When you're successful, the world takes notice. Your best defense against competitors is to keep improving the idea with the same innovation that got you there. They can copy you, but they can't keep up with you.

Your Audacious Promise

Stop and ask yourself this question—what is your audacious promise?

Why should someone buy your product, attend your event, join your cause, shop at your store, or read your book? What great hope do you have to offer them?

At Starbucks, it's about experiencing the community of an Italian espresso shop. At Disney, it's about making dreams come true for the child in you. At Apple, it's about using a computer without a learning curve. At Harley-Davidson, it's that even you can be a badass.

But what is yours?

Carrie Starr joined Dream Year in 2012 with an audacious promise for young married couples. Carrie and her husband are professors at a college in upstate New York and mentor a lot of young adults in their careers and relationships.

You owe it to us all to get on with what you're good at.

—W. H. AUDEN

They believe in the importance of a strong marriage and have seen the consequences of not starting out with a solid foundation. Between Carrie and her husband, their parents have been married six times. So Carrie's audacious promise is to help young couples make their first marriage their only one.

Carrie launched Marriage Adventures, which is an organization that offers resources and retreats to help young couples stay married for life. The Starrs even offer up their beautiful country farm as an affordable site to host weddings.

What audacious promise does your dream offer?

The Monkey Project promises to give women and children in Peru a better life with each purchase of a lovable monkey. Netflix promises that you can keep your video for as long as you'd like without any penalty. Secret Cinema promises, not just a great movie, but a wonderful surprise experience as well. And Zipcar promises you don't have to own or rent a car to be a driver for a few hours.

Find Your Formula

Your dream needs a model that "clicks" with customers. It's a unique formula that attracts followers and makes people exclaim, "Why didn't I think of that?"

Finding a successful formula is no easy task. It's like trying to open a combination lock when you don't know the numbers. But rest assured—there is a formula. And you can find it through careful observation, research, and experimentation. If you keep turning the tumblers, you'll eventually crack the code.

In 2007, Andrew Mason from Chicago started a Web site called The Point, which tried to mobilize groups of people to help charitable causes. The projects required a minimum number of participants to commit their time or money to a cause before the project was green-lit. If the cause didn't attract enough participants, the project was scrapped. If it reached its goal, the project "tipped" and was undertaken by those who backed it.

The trouble was—tips rarely happened. Not enough people got behind the projects to mobilize them. "It was a big abstract idea that wasn't getting any traction," Andrew said. "So we tried to focus on one specific way that people were using the site. Group buying seemed to be the most promising."

In an effort to find a more successful model, Andrew launched a new site in November 2008 that offered group-based discounts on products. It was the same concept as The Point but sold coupons instead of volunteerism. For example, you could get two pizzas for the price of one if enough people signed up. Another deal sold time in a sensory deprivation chamber.

Andrew's second idea took off immediately and became the fastest-growing business in global history. You know the Web site as Groupon, which reached a billion dollars in sales in just two years. Services have expanded to five hundred markets and 35 million registered users.

Andrew Mason found his formula.

Turning the tumblers could be one factor; it could be a series of factors; but you have to adjust the model until you "crack the code."

I fear not the man who practiced ten thousand kicks one time, but I fear the man who has practiced one kick ten thousand times.

—BRUCE LEE

The code is the unique imprint of your offering. It's what makes the dream work. It could be your pricing model. It could be the personality of your brand. It could be how you treat customers, the quality of your materials, or the style of your work. But it's where your offering meets the fascination of other people. It's the distinct way in which you make your offering available to the world.

The New Yorker profiled Reed Krakoff, who left Coach handbags to launch his own luxury brand. Reed described the "code" that allowed him to take Coach from $500 million in earnings to $4 billion in just fifteen years: "I bang it out. I know what came before, I know what's coming next; I know how it will work in the context of the store and the ads. It's like a code."

The article went on to say that "after fifteen years, Krakoff speaks the Coach code so fluently that when he says 'I like that one' in a design meeting, he isn't expressing personal appreciation of a stripe, a shape, or a zipper.'" He likes it because he knows "it's doing what it's supposed to do."

Some people get lucky and crack the code on their first attempt. Some people discover the code only after years of unsuccessful attempts. And others find the formula by studying the successes of others.

But there is a code, and it's up to you to crack it.

In June 2009, *USA Today* interviewed novelist John Grisham's close friend Bill Ballard, who was the second person to read his first manuscript, *A Time to Kill*. Bill described how John came up with a winning formula for great story lines:

"He analyzed how bestsellers were constructed, plot development, at what time readers would be engaged, and at what time they would put the book down," Bill said. "He knows the last page of the book when he starts writing the first one."

In other words, when John Grisham writes, he follows a formula. He knows how to create a gripping plot, the right chapter-by-chapter progression, how to introduce characters, and the best way to end the story on the final page. This formula has sold more than 250 million books worldwide.

You are already predisposed to a formula. The question is whether it's the right one. You have to keep adjusting it until you find the one that works.

In his book *Linchpin*, Seth Godin writes about artists who refuse to adapt their formulas: "One author I know is willing to watch his books sit unsold, because that's a better outcome to him than changing the essence of what he's written. He has a passion for his craft, but no real passion for spreading his ideas."

If our ideas aren't spreading, it's not other people's fault. If they're not buying it or reading it or attending it or giving to it or embracing it, there's only one thing to blame: the formula. Our job is to keep adjusting it until we hear the sweet "clicking" sound of success.

Call to Action

The trouble with ideas is that everyone has them. In fact, many people have *your* idea, which means your dream doesn't have a shot. The solution is to create a new "idea model." This is an idea presented in a different way—a way that's never been done before. You can't find it from inspiration. You can't find it from copying other people. You have to identify the "rules" of your industry and break them.

The first step in creating an idea model is to compare your dream with all of the other offerings in your field. If it's not a starkly unique idea, hardly anyone will notice it. They're too busy to explore all of the similar options. They'll simply choose the most popular option.

If there's already a clear leader in your field, there's no room for a wannabe version. You have to be the alternative. You have to be the "anti-them." You have to be the thing for people who don't like *the other* thing or you'll be overlooked, forgotten, or ignored. Take, for instance, the pest control companies Orkin and Terminix. In Orkin commercials, bugs always get to drive off in insect cars and live while Terminix enforces complete and total annihilation. They both appeal to a very different customer base—those who have empathy for insects and those who don't.

Next, write down all of the conventions or "rules" of your industry. These are the ways organizations act because that's the way it's always been done. For example, chiropractors tend to close their offices for several hours each day for an extended lunch break. Pizza shops tend to make circular pies with similar ingredients. And dry cleaners tend to accommodate shoppers on the go.

But why?

Try breaking the rules in a calculated, thoughtful way. Go through each rule in your industry and ask why it's done that way. Some rules are there for a reason, but others can be violated to produce a better result.

Describe your idea model below. It doesn't have to be proven. But don't go forward without being able to express it in a few sentences.

QUESTIONS:

1. In an age of oversaturation, successful ideas require new models. What innovations can you bring to your industry?
2. What is the audacious promise that your dream is making?
3. How can you test your idea model in a smaller, less risky way before investing more resources?

YOUR FINANCIAL MODEL

It'll cost you everything to dream, and everything not to.
....
—REVEREND RUN

Your Dream Is Not a Hobby

Dream Year is about pursuing your passion. But it's also about creating a financially sustainable idea. The goal is not merely to do something audacious but to create revenue that will provide income for you, generate a profit, and allow you to benefit others if you'd like.

If you're not concerned about creating revenue, it's not a dream. It's a hobby. And it's okay to have hobbies, but pursuing a dream is about sustaining your ideas so you can continue to bring your gift to the world.

Make no mistake about it—whether your dream is nonprofit or for-profit, a book or a bookstore, your goal is to make a profit.

I've heard countless people blame their financial woes on being a nonprofit organization. But being nonprofit doesn't mean you're supposed to hurt for money. That's not a requirement. You don't have to beg for donations, struggle to survive, and bring in less money than for-profits. I know plenty of nonprofits that make more money than for-profits. The point of being nonprofit is that no one can personally profit from the organization, and it must engage in activities that fall within the IRS's guidelines for a tax-exempt organization. It doesn't mean the organization can't make a profit. In fact, it needs to make as much as it spends or more in order to keep operating.

Some of us have trouble charging money for our dreams. Maybe we think the work is too enjoyable to get paid for it. Or maybe we're unsure of the value it brings to other people. But most of us have exactly the income we have because somewhere along the way, we settled for it. We decided that this amount was good enough for now, and we put our ambitions in park.

Business author Barbara Stanny describes how we land in this rut:

- We tolerate low pay in favor of other perks or less work.
- We're lousy negotiators, reluctant to ask for more.
- We believe in the nobility of poverty, repeating the cycle.
- We are subtle self-saboteurs, always stopping short of our goals.
- We sacrifice our dreams for the preferences of others.
- We live in financial chaos with no plan or organization.

Your dream is about reviving a great vision for your life. It's about expanding how you see yourself and what you're capable of achieving. Accepting money for your dream might feel uncomfortable at first, but it's critical to your success.

A New Way of Looking at Money

No one trains us to pursue our dreams. So we come at the world with the mind-set of an employee, not knowing that we can—or are allowed to—pursue our own ideas. We apply for jobs, go to school to get better jobs, and vote for presidents who promise more jobs.

It's not until some catalytic moment happens that our perspective shifts from employee to entrepreneur. It could be a bad boss, a layoff from work, a good book, a recreational venture that succeeds, or an encounter with someone who inspires us to change our thinking.

For Jeff Bezos, the founder of Amazon, it came as a teenager from a bad summer job at McDonald's. For James Cameron, the director of *Avatar* and *Titanic*, it came from watching *Star Wars* in a movie theater.

For me, it came from working in the seafood department at a grocery store when I was sixteen years old. I'll never forget coming home each night reeking of shellfish. My clothes and the interior of my car were ruined after just one week. It finally dawned on me that if I depended on jobs for money, I was never going to do what I loved.

> There's nothing wrong with a paycheck, unless it interferes with your ability to earn what you're worth. It usually does.
>
> —T. HARV EKER

So I bought a lawn mower for $200 and a thousand business cards for $50 and plastered the neighborhood with offers for my lawn care service. Each time I got a customer, I would cut the grass twice—once in one direction and once in the other—just to outperform the competition. I did so well each summer that I didn't have to work the other eight months out of the year. I've been a dream chaser ever since.

By learning how to take an initial investment of $250 and turn it into a profitable financial model, I was doing exactly what the grocery store had done to create a job for me, albeit on a smaller scale. But being able to earn my own way proved that I could do what I wanted and still make money from it.

Money doesn't only come from conventional employer relationships. You don't have to exchange the best years of your life in a cubicle for a paycheck. It is entirely possible for you to wake up each day and do what you love.

But you have to look at money through a different lens. Most employees are clueless about the flow of cash in and out of an organization.

A dream chaser is never clueless about money.

A Great Idea Is a Spreadsheet with Skin On

Your dream can have terrific branding, great customer service, a nice location, and wonderful offerings. But if you spend more money than you take in, your dream will fail. Organizations go broke all the time because they get the spreadsheet wrong.

How many times have you driven past a favorite retail establishment only to be surprised one day by an empty storefront? Nobody saw it coming except the business owner and the accountant.

Behind every amusement park, feature film, music project, charitable organization, ministry, or restaurant, there is a spreadsheet. And without a profitable one, these gifts cannot be enjoyed by the world. No cause for social justice can be sustained. No piece of art can come to life. And your ideas will be stuck in your head, rather than living in the real world where they belong.

You might be thinking *I don't want to think about money! I want to focus on the dream! I just want to write or design or sing or make pies!*

But the record label sees your music as a financial investment. The publisher has financial metrics to decide whether they'll publish your book. The pie shop can't stay in business for long if the ingredients, payroll, and rent cost more than the pies bring in. Until you come to see the financial framework that underlies your dream, it will have all of the organizational fortitude of a piñata.

Bold action in the face of uncertainty is not only terrifying, but necessary in the pursuit of great work.

—JONATHAN FIELDS

Even Cirque du Soleil discards great ideas that aren't profitable. President Daniel Lamarre described three criteria for any creative endeavor they pursue:

1. It must be a creative challenge.
2. It must have creative partners.
3. And it must be profitable.

If you are going to pursue your dream, you can no longer see yourself as merely the practitioner of the idea. You are now the chief financial officer as well. No one else but you will care about the spreadsheet.

Construct a Financial Model

Before you pursue your dream, construct a financial model for it. You have to know what you're up against. Everything has a financial model—books, churches, businesses, nonprofits, and even your own household. But no matter how many zeroes are in your numbers or how many categories of spending you have, there is just one model. And it is a very simple formula:

Revenue

– Expenses

= Profit or Loss

Dreams rise and fall on this formula.

For you to continue bringing your gift to the world, the revenue must be greater than the expenses. If it's not, the model won't work. And a nonworking model is a nonworking model, regardless of what you're trying to accomplish.

This is too important to screw up. If you can't get your dream to work on a spreadsheet, it won't work in the real world.

Here are some questions to ask:

1. How much revenue can you generate with this idea?
2. What are the sources of revenue? Can you create others?

3. How much will your expenses be? How can you reduce them?
4. What is the total amount of profit after expenses are paid?
5. Is the profit worth the amount of work it will take?
6. How long can you survive if you don't make a profit right away?

Creating a financial model won't guarantee your success, but it will show you how the organization could potentially operate. It will show you where the money is coming from and where it's going out. It will tell you whether you can afford to quit your job or whether you have to work a second one.

This due diligence will shore up the loose corners of your dream. It will make you more financially responsible and define the financial activity of your organization. It will show you, quite frankly, if your dream is viable.

The revenue will give you a goal to pursue. The expenses will put a limit on how much you can spend. And when the real numbers start coming in, the totals had better match up or you'll need to change the plan in order to stay in business.

Duy Nguyen joined Dream Year in 2011 to help his struggling restaurant become profitable. He owned an Asian-fusion café called Ozen in downtown Quebec. Duy's restaurant was losing money every month. His expenses were greater than his revenue.

The first thing I did was look at his spreadsheet. I wanted to see the health of his financial model. Duy provided several months of statements, and I could immediately see the problem. His numbers were spread across several tabs and I couldn't see clear categories for revenue and expenses. He was using the spreadsheet to report numbers from each day's sales and expenses, but he wasn't using it to control his financial activity.

A financial model is meant to guide your activity, not just report it. Think of it as a road map to follow. It allows the business to control the numbers, rather than let the numbers control the business. Basic bookkeeping with QuickBooks or a similar program can help you track your activity. But a financial model predicts how the organization will function. It defines what revenue must come in to cover the expenses before anything actually happens.

Together, Duy and I created a new financial model that organized his expenses into categories, such as rent, food costs, payroll, and so on. Then we broke down his revenue into measurable categories, such as lunch sales, dinner sales, catering, and carryout platters. We looked at which categories were performing well and which ones needed to be discarded, altered, or strengthened. Essentially, we constructed a new business model while the current one was operating.

The result was a beautiful, easy-to-read formula that enabled Duy to control his financial results and not live in the dark about why his business was hemorrhaging every month. By sticking to these parameters, Duy was able to report a profit within three months. One year later, he opened two more locations.

The financial model held all of the secrets.

How Will You Create Revenue?

By now, you should know your idea model—or the primary activity of your dream. Before we go any further, let's figure out how this activity will create revenue.

If you're a cook, will you open a restaurant or cater meals for private dinner parties? Will you produce your own cookbook or will you package your best dish for supermarket shelves? There are multiple ways to express your gift.

Chef Frances Kroner in Cincinnati started a project called Feast, which she describes as a pop-up restaurant in people's homes. She cooks dinner for up to twenty-four people, charging the host for the number of guests. The menus are four to six courses with an emphasis on local, seasonal, and organic meat and produce.

If you're a fashion designer, will you create a line of clothing to sell in retail stores? Will you set up your own online shop? Or will you start a nonprofit that secures donations and grants for teaching fashion design to inner-city youth? Revenue could come from clothing sales or charitable donations.

Once you define the activity of your dream, determine how that activity will generate revenue. What are the possible sources of income?

It might take a few attempts to discover the best revenue stream. People won't pay for something they don't want. But if you keep experimenting, you'll find your audience. This process is called "customer creation."

Customer Creation

You'd think Hollywood existed to create great movies. Just watch the Academy Awards. It celebrates the best films that studios can produce. But in his book *The Hollywood Economist*, journalist Edward Jay Epstein gives us a different take.

In 1929, four fifths of the population went to movies. But today, with so many competing options for entertainment, only 10 percent of the population goes to movie theaters. It's a dying industry and one that can no longer exist purely for the sake of making great films. Studios have had to find a more profitable purpose.

This objective has become "customer creation." It's where you discover what people want first and then shape your offering around those preferences.

Films are no longer green-lit based on the story or the idea, but rather on their marketability. Is there a customer base for it? As it turns out, the most likely people to attend movies on weekends are teenagers, which is why you see so many raunchy and irreverent releases coming out of Tinseltown.

Let me ask you a question. What would you do if you were the Chief Customer Creation Officer for your dream? How would you align the activity of your dream with what people want? Your ideas can serve a great purpose, but if they fail to connect with people, they'll do very little good.

Make It Easy for People to Buy

Once you create something people want, make it easy for them to buy it. They may like the overall idea, but if it's too hard to purchase, too expensive, or they don't understand what you're offering, they'll walk away.

Your job is to make it easy for them to say yes.

Start by creating "packages" they can understand.

Katie Strandlund from Nashville started volunteering at my STORY conference in 2010 and quickly discovered that she was good at organizing events. She knew how to manage all of the complex logistics to help them run smoothly.

As Katie started getting paid for her work, she wanted to add more clients but had a difficult time describing what she did to other people. We were having a conversation one day when it became clear that she was gifted at doing all of the administrative things that other people didn't like to do—the "dirty work."

So she called her new company "Dirty Work" and designed three packages at varying price points. She could coordinate an entire event, manage short-term projects, or serve as an executive assistant. Katie could do more than these three things of course. But by creating easy-to-understand packages, she made it easy for clients to say yes. She filled her client roster in no time.

Hilary Barnett from Nashville did the same thing with her social media skills. She started out by maintaining STORY's Twitter account. In just six months, she doubled the number of followers and figured out how to schedule an entire week's worth of tweets in just a few hours. It was a reproducible system.

So Hilary designed several packages under the brand "Savvee" that enabled clients to purchase her services at several different price points. She could do as little as manage a Twitter account, write more substantive content, such as blog posts and press releases, or run an entire communications strategy.

Creating packages isn't just for service work. Matt Cote joined Dream Year in 2012 to start a new ministry in the Boston area. He needed $100,000 in donations. But rather than letting people choose from unlimited giving options, which can paralyze their decision making, he created a package called "100 Strong" that asked one hundred people to give $100 a month for a year. It gave supporters a compelling identity and an easy way to say yes.

Levels of Engagement

In order to grow your revenue, you'll want to create packages at increasing levels that help people say yes to larger offerings. It's much easier for people to spend more money with you when they're already customers. You've earned their trust.

Don't make the mistake of creating only one expensive package that forces customers to decide whether they're in or they're out. The price point will become a barrier to entry. Some people need to "wade into the pool." They need a way to engage with your brand before purchasing a high-end package.

The solution is to create "levels of engagement."

Imagine an inverted triangle or a funnel. At the top of the funnel—its widest point—come up with a free offer for your idea model. This could be a monthly e-newsletter, a blog, a podcast, a PDF book, or a trial. It's a way for people to become fans without becoming customers yet.

The next stage of the funnel represents a moderate price point. Fewer people will participate at this level than the free level, but it enables them to buy something from you without going all in. If you're an interior designer, it could be an online course for $149.99. If you're a business consultant, it could be a weekend seminar where multiple people participate at a lower price point than one-on-one coaching.

At the bottom of your funnel is the "all in" version of your idea model. This is for the raving fans of your organization. It's your highest price point and the fullest expression of your dream. This is ultimately what you want all of your customers to do. But having a funnel allows people to engage with you no matter how much money they can pay.

Creating multiple levels of engagement applies to any industry and any kind of dream. If you're a nonprofit, you can create multiple donor packages. If you're a design firm or a photography studio, you can create multiple service packages. If you're a restaurant, you can offer various dining packages. But each level beckons users to take one step deeper into the funnel. It allows them to "wade into the pool" so they can eventually end up in the deep end.

A Portfolio of Revenue

Your dream can have more than one income stream. Your success doesn't depend on just one offering. You can create a "portfolio of revenue" that generates income from different sources. Just as a mutual fund balances the highs and lows of individual stocks, your dream will be more sustainable by diversifying the sources of income.

For example, if you own a hair salon, you will obviously generate revenue from haircuts, but don't forget about product sales, spa treatments, pedicures, product sponsorships, and even spray tans.

A San Diego–based road race organizer called Competitor Group has figured out how to create multiple revenue streams from running events. They charge entry fees for several types of courses including mud races and rock-and-roll marathons. But they also generate revenue from these additional offerings:

- Corporate sponsorships
- Training programs for upcoming races
- Travel commissions from flights, hotels, and car rentals
- Documentary photography packages for runners
- Sales from running apparel
- Discounted entry fees on future races

Who said you could only make money from one source? Chances are you'll need multiple sources in order to stay in business.

John Saddington in Atlanta has worked his way into becoming a "professional blogger." When we hear this term, we typically think of one revenue source—advertisements. But John shared his secret sauce, and it's multiple revenue streams. Here are the sources of income he listed on his blog:

1. Direct advertising sales
2. Advertising networks
3. Affiliate marketing
4. Paid reviews and sponsored posts
5. Blog networks, guest and paid postings
6. Selling products, merchandise, and expertise
7. Big business and corporate blogging
8. Services and business development
9. Premium content, auxiliary sites, donations, and more

It turns out that much of John's revenue as a "professional blogger" comes from a portfolio of revenue—building Web sites, offering consulting services, selling products, and ghost-blogging for other people, among many other things.

It doesn't matter what industry you're in, you can create multiple revenue streams by partitioning your dream into categories.

Let's revisit the photography business. You could expand your revenue beyond photography packages to include picture-frame sales, styling and wardrobe services, premium holiday packages, and custom photo albums. As a successful photographer, you might even sell an instructional course on how to build a photography business.

One of the ways Duy Nguyen improved his restaurant was by strengthening his portfolio of revenue. He agreed to close out his registers every day at four P.M. so we could make a clear distinction between lunch and dinner sales. Ozen had a strong lunchtime clientele, but when we separated the revenue into multiple categories, it was easy to see that dinnertime was struggling.

So Duy began experimenting with ways to grow the evening crowd. He dimmed the lights, changed the music, and added new items to the menu. He even started rewarding lunchtime customers with dinner coupons. By isolating and enhancing the dinnertime service at his restaurant, Duy was able to increase his evening sales.

Now instead of monitoring just one revenue source, Duy analyzes lunch sales, dinner sales, catering sales, and take-out sales. He treats them like separate business units so he can improve and grow each one.

Invent New Revenue Streams

Whenever you create new revenue streams, you not only improve your financial results; you also innovate your industry.

In 2012, comedian Louis C.K. bypassed the cable networks to offer his own live show on the Internet for $5 per person. With this offering, he became the talent, the producer, and the distribution channel all in one. He shook up the stand-up comedy industry by cutting out the promoter and going straight to the customer. In the first four days, he sold 110,000 subscriptions for a total of $550,000. Now other comedians, such as Jim Gaffigan, are offering their own shows for $5 on the Internet as well.

At Dream Year Weekends, I conduct an exercise in which participants are asked to rethink the financial model of a lemonade stand. They're not allowed to charge money for the lemonade, so they have to find other sources of revenue. Popular ideas have included flavored ice, souvenir cups, and delivery charges. It's easier to come up with new revenue streams when you exclude the obvious one.

Try this same exercise with your own idea model. Let's say you can't charge money for your primary offering. How else could you make money? Then add it to your portfolio of revenue.

This is exactly what happened in 2009, when Garrett Camp and Travis Kalanick launched Uber. They created a mobile app that connects passengers with drivers of vehicles for hire. Using a smartphone, riders can signal the nearest cab or black car to pick them up at their GPS location.

Uber doesn't own any cars. They're not a cab company. In fact, Uber skirts city laws that prohibit unlicensed taxicabs by qualifying as a car-for-hire service, which has fewer restrictions. Uber earns a fee for taking online reservations, which is something the cab industry has never done before. And it's quite a fee. In December 2013, a leaked financial statement showed that Uber made $19 million a week.

Brainstorming revenue models is a great way to create a revolutionary new idea model. By changing how you make money, you can change the industry.

Andy Hargadon of UC Davis is an expert on cross-disciplinary entrepreneurship and the author of *How Breakthroughs Happen: The Surprising Truth About How Companies Innovate*. He describes eight revenue models to consider:

1. Unit sales—selling products or services
2. Advertising fees—selling message space on your site

ZUMBA'S PORTFOLIO OF REVENUE

Zumba is one of the fastest-growing fitness companies in history, offering its fashionable, dance-crazed aerobics to enthusiasts all over the world. The company grew 4,000 percent from 2007 to 2010 and 750 percent from 2011 to 2012.

Here are the sources of revenue:

- Class fees of $4 to $20 for students
- DVDs, Xbox games, and iTunes music
- Fitness concerts with an average ticket price of $40
- Fitness clothing line
- Instruction conventions at a cost of $499 each
- Instructor licensing at an average fee of $250 each
- Memberships of $30 a month to be in the Zumba Instructor Network

3. Franchise fees—selling someone the right to expand your business
4. Utility fees—selling goods and services on a per-use basis
5. Subscription fees—selling monthly or yearly access
6. Transaction fees—selling a fee for enabling a transaction
7. Professional fees—selling your time
8. Licensing fees—selling the rights to use intellectual property

This isn't a comprehensive list. Innovators are coming up with new revenue streams all the time. But it will help get you started as you brainstorm your own financial model.

Calculate Your Expenses

Now that you've determined how you'll create revenue and the packages (or levels of engagement) you'll offer, let's figure out the costs to deliver it.

Write down every conceivable expense that's associated with delivering your product or service. This is more than a financial exercise. It will force you to define the system of your organization—how you produce what you do.

If you're a photographer, you might have three packages—the "candid" session for $250, the "posed" session for $500, and the "studio" session for $750. Let's say each package comes with digital images from the shoot and several prints.

If you already own the equipment, your costs will include traveling to locations, the cost of the prints, the materials for the final product, and your own time. You could save time by hiring an editor to improve the photos as a part of your expenses. And don't forget the cost of the binder or frames to present your finished product.

Once you calculate all of the expenses, subtract them from your projected revenue and see what's left. You'll notice that some packages might be more profitable than others. If they're all profitable, you're in good shape. But if you're losing money on any one of them, there are three options available:

1. Raise your prices.
2. Find a way to decrease your costs until you're profitable.
3. Get rid of the unprofitable options and find new ones.

Reduce Expenses

There are two ways to have a more profitable financial model. One is to increase your revenue (more customers or higher prices). The other is to reduce expenses.

You don't need that ergonomically correct Aeron office chair just yet. In fact, you don't even need an office. Use the free Wi-Fi at Starbucks. Hire freelancers, not employees. Keep pushing your outdated laptop for as long as it can go.

Fashion maven Kate Spade confessed that when she launched her first line of handbags, she couldn't afford the elaborate booth setups of other brands at trade shows. So she crafted a shabby chic exhibit with fake grass and lawn furniture that she found at thrift stores. It saved her money and grabbed attention.

When Brandon McCormick started his film company Whitestone Motion Pictures in Atlanta, he couldn't afford to do sound recording at first, so he wrote screenplays that didn't require dialogue. It became a hallmark of his early short films and forced him to focus on writing better story lines.

> If it's important to you, you'll find a way. If it's not, you'll find an excuse.
>
> —JIM ROHN

You can reduce your costs. It just takes discipline and a little creativity. The trick is to reduce your expenses without hindering the quality of your work. Someone once said, "There is fast; there is cheap; and there is good. You can only have two out of three."

Another way to reduce expenses is to find partners who will share the costs.

In the first few years of STORY, I partnered with magazines to promote the event in exchange for subscription offers to my attendees. I partnered with publishing companies to put speakers onstage for a sponsorship fee. I partnered with record labels to put bands onstage. And I partnered with audio-visual companies to get production gear in exchange for promotion. In most cases, these companies offered free services or paid the fees of their talent in exchange for the promotional value that I offered at the event. I saved hundreds of thousands of dollars in those early years by finding organizations to split the costs.

How could you benefit by partnering with other organizations? How could they benefit by partnering with you? Is it worth a trade?

How to Set a Price

Setting a price begins with calculating your operational expenses, from the postage stamps and office supplies to your Internet service and monthly paycheck. Leave no stone unturned or the overlooked costs will eat into your profit. All of these expenses amount to your "cost of goods sold." You should know exactly how much each product, each customer, each attendee, or each performance costs you. Once these costs are established, you can set a price to determine your profit margin—or the difference between what your customers pay and the cost to deliver it.

Choosing the right price comes from trial and error. If you've been in the industry for a while, you'll know how to price things. But if you're new or starting something that's never been done before, you'll have to guess. There's no manual that tells you what the price should be. You have to figure it out.

Fast food restaurants do this all the time with new items. In 2012, Taco Bell, which offers tacos for $.89, introduced a steak cantina bowl for $4.99 to see if people would go for it. McDonald's supplemented its $.50 apple pies by adding $1.89 vanilla bean scones to the menu. And Wendy's upgraded its $1.49 garden side salad to a $6.99 berry almond chicken salad as an experiment.

In the military, they call this "bracketing the target." Artillery gunners find a target by shooting just to the left and then to the right of it until they find the exact center. You can do this with pricing as well. If you aim too low, you might not cover your costs and you'll have more customers than you can handle. Small businesses get overrun all the time by offering extreme discounts. And if you aim too high, no one will buy it. Either way, you'll find the "true price" by repackaging it and offering it again at an improved price point.

The price is not just the cost of the offering. You add value with the experience, the exclusivity, the uniqueness, and even the story behind your brand. The same factory in Israel that makes Jordache jeans also makes jeans for Levi's. It's just a different label on the back. They can sell them at different price points because of where they sell them, the branding, and the customers they target.

Journalist Rob Walker created an experimental site called SignificantObjects.com where he demonstrates how the power of story can affect price. Rob goes shopping at thrift stores, garage sales, and flea markets, buying products for just a few dollars. Then he writes a fictitious story about each product and uploads it to eBay. On average, the original cost of these objects is $1.29 and the resale price after adding a story is $36.12. In one case, an author named Blake Butler bought a snow globe with Utah printed on the side for 99 cents. After writing a fantastical and somewhat ridiculous story about finding the globe among his grandfather's possessions, he sold it for $59.

Offering a unique experience is another powerful value addition. Business consultant Neil Baron wrote about the pricing strategy of a retail store called Harvey's Hardware in his town of Needham, Massachusetts. He noted four interesting things about Harvey's:

1. They never have the lowest prices.
2. They never run a sale.
3. They never provide discounts or coupons.
4. They limit their advertising to the back of Little League uniforms.

Neil explained how they're able to charge so much and still thrive in business. Harvey's provides a unique experience that you can't get anywhere else. First, a salesperson greets you at the door. She doesn't ask what you need but to describe the problem you're trying to solve. The salesperson then finds the materials or tools while you wait. She explains how to solve your problem and then helps carry the items to your car if needed. At Harvey's, you're not just buying a tool or a light fixture. You're buying an experience. And people gladly pay a premium to have it.

Raising Start-up Funds

I'm not a fan of investor capital. Finding investors sounds glamorous. Their seed money can help accelerate your growth. It can take the pressure off your cash flow, and you can get valuable advice and connections from business experts. But when someone else funds your dream, you give up control.

Control belongs to those who write the checks.

If you want your book to be published, you'll no longer own your own book. The publisher will. They can change the content to suit their tastes. And if you want copies of your own book, you'll have to purchase them like everyone else.

If you want to have your screenplay produced, a studio will buy your script. They can change all of the Hondas to Chevrolets and put someone else's name on it if they want to because they own it now. You sold your dream.

In their book *Rework*, authors Jason Fried and David Heinemeier Hansson dismiss the idea that you need investors: "Far too often, people think the answer is to raise money from outsiders. If you're building something like a factory or a restaurant, then you may indeed need that outside cash. But a lot of companies don't need expensive infrastructure—especially these days. We're in a service economy now. Service businesses . . . don't require much to get going."

You can fund your own dream. You can put aside money each month, open a credit line at the bank, apply for a small business loan or a grant, borrow it from your friends, sell your unneeded furniture on Craigslist; and if you still don't have the money, work a second job.

A friend of mine owned a start-up technology company that was running low on cash. They couldn't survive without additional capital, but he didn't want to give up ownership to an investor. So my friend offered his programming services for a season to a large bank on the West Coast to raise additional funds. This account had nothing to do with his core business, but it brought in several hundred thousand dollars' worth of capital he could use for his project—no strings attached. My friend found a way to raise money for his start-up without giving up equity.

How to Find Investors

If you choose to find investors, let me explain how to do it. There are no rules, no guidelines to follow, and no protocols to keep. It is an act of negotiation. In other words, you get the deal that you can get.

A friend of mine in Knoxville, Tennessee, wanted to buy a prop airplane for his own leisure, but he couldn't afford to buy it himself. So he invited six friends to his house for dinner and proposed an idea.

He divided the cost of the plane by six, added the monthly maintenance fees, and proposed a flight schedule so they could all use the plane in a time-share. Five of his friends bought in at a slightly higher amount, and all of them became the proud owners of a new plane. It was a simple way to share the risk of a venture. And the return on the investment was the thrill of flying.

In a similar way, here's how to find capital for your dream:

1. Identify potential investors.

These could include businesspeople, friends with discretionary income, fathers-in-law, or even a venture capital firm. People love a good investment opportunity.

2. Cast vision for the project.

Invite them to hear about your idea and what you hope to accomplish. Let them know the problem you're trying to solve and how you know there's demand for it.

3. Explain your idea model.

Explain how the model works, how you'll market it, and how you plan to deliver the offering. Lay out the system for how it works from start to finish.

4. Present a financial model.

Create a financial model that projects revenue and expenses over the next several years. Do the research, and offer your best prediction for profitability.

5. Make an offer for return on investment.

Will you give them 40 percent equity for $20,000 or 10 percent? There's no rule here. Find an arrangement that suits you both. The worst they can do is say no.

These people are investing in your business, for sure, but even more, they're investing in you. They want to see your passion, your work ethic, your track record, and whether you've got skin in the game.

Give them a reason to believe in you.

Once you find investors, you'll need to draw up a contract and establish a reporting system for the sake of accountability. I recommend consulting an attorney and an accountant before pitching any investors at all, as there will be legal ramifications to consider up front.

If you approach a venture capital firm, they often have their own process for presenting ideas. And it usually requires an introduction from someone who has been successfully funded or is a part of their network to get an audience. But this is a great opportunity to refine your idea with their feedback and make a big ask.

Call to Action

A great idea is a spreadsheet with skin on. In other words, it doesn't matter how great your idea might seem. If it's not financially sustainable, you'll never be able to continue bringing it to the world. While finances might stress out some people, a dream chaser cannot afford to be clueless about money. You must be the financial architect of your dream. But have no fear. The formula never gets more complicated than this—your revenue must be greater than or equal to your expenses.

The next step in realizing your dream is creating a financial model for it. That is, you must take your idea model and put numbers to it. What are the activities of your model? Do you bake pies? Do you deliver pies? Do you travel and sell your pies to grocery stores? Whatever the activities might be, list the costs of doing them. These are your expenses.

Now project how much revenue you can make. If your revenue is not greater than your costs, you either need to increase revenue, reduce expenses, or find a whole new model altogether. And don't stop with one source. A successful dream comes from a portfolio of revenue. You'll need multiple income streams to make the most of your dream and guard against the downfall of a single source.

Before you go any further, create a financial model for your dream. List your portfolio of revenue at the top and calculate the expenses below to see if it's viable. Keep working at it until you're happy with it. Plan the work and then go work the plan.

QUESTIONS:

1. Create a portfolio of revenue for your dream. What other sources of revenue can you create besides your primary offering?

2. What partners might consider helping you develop your dream? How could they benefit from working with you and help you reduce costs?

3. Before you look for investor capital, have you exhausted all of the opportunities to fund your own dream? If so, who could you approach?

EXECUTING THE DREAM

The best time to plant a tree was twenty years ago.
The next best time is now.
—CHINESE PROVERB

A System Whereby a Dream Results

Several years ago, I was looking through best-selling leadership author John Maxwell's video library when I came across a lesson called "How I Write" and was forever changed by what I saw.

John was sitting in his office—or some facsimile in a studio—with a yellow legal pad in front of him. He said, "I've been approached by hundreds of people who ask me how I'm able to write all of these books. Today, I want to tell you how I write. I simply sit down with a pen and a pad of paper and I write."

He went on to explain that most people never write because they never actually write. They dream of writing. They talk about writing. But they never take the time to do it. As someone who had dreamed of writing a book for years, I was stopped cold by this obvious truth.

I had a ton of great book ideas. I had even imagined their covers. In fact, I was planning to write one just as soon as I could afford four months' stay at a beachside resort where I supposed great books get written. But deep down, I knew that was never going to happen.

I preferred the inspiration to the perspiration.

Leaving work that day, I realized I had been carrying around a dream but had never done the work to make it happen. When I got home, I coordinated with my wife, Ainsley, to set aside several four-hour blocks of time throughout the week to write while our children were napping.

From December to June, I went to Starbucks three days a week to write whether I wanted to or not. And I'm proud to tell you that from this arduous, unwavering schedule, a book resulted. It had nothing to do with inspiration, great ideas, or some special talent for writing. It happened because I set a schedule.

There is something glorious about an unexecuted dream. It's easy. It exists perfectly in our minds. And we can dream about it all we like without ever breaking a sweat. But great ideas have no value unless they're executed.

Your vision has a dark side. The minute you start pursuing it, the burden becomes bigger than the idea. Your dream offers more pain than euphoria. At times, you'll wonder why you started in the first place. This is why you need a system—a system whereby your dream will result.

It could be a schedule you keep, an outline you complete, or a plan you follow. But unless you show up for work, it won't happen.

A system walks you through the hardship. It shows you how to move toward the goal by putting one foot in front of the other. A system keeps you going when the inspiration is gone (and believe me—it will leave you).

There are no such things as successful visionaries, only architects of successful vision-producing systems.

To create a system for achieving your dream, start from its completed form in your mind's eye and work backward. Plot the steps from start to finish. Forget about the first frame of your movie. Don't worry about the opening line of your book. Start at the very end. Write the conclusion and the steps it takes to get there. Have the vision to see your dream fully realized, and then create the schedule or the system to get there.

This is the process. And it's what separates the dreamers from the doers.

The Importance of Starting

If your dream exists only in your mind, it's invisible to the rest of the world. This is why starting is so important. One of the interesting outcomes in going after your dream is that people find out what you're capable of doing only after you do it. Until then, no one has a clue about your potential.

Just start. You don't even have to succeed. Fail gloriously if needed. But the very act of starting will bring your dream to the surface.

> The cost of being wrong is less than the cost of doing nothing.
>
> —SETH GODIN

In 2007, Justin Kan started a Web-based television show called Justin.tv with the help of a $50,000 check from the venture capitalists at Y Combinator. The idea was to broadcast a live video channel twenty-four hours a day, seven days a week and generate revenue from advertisers.

When producing just one show proved to be financially unsustainable, Justin turned it into a platform that would feature other live channels.

Justin admits that he made a lot of mistakes at the beginning. He didn't have a plan for scaling the site. He didn't know anything about the broadcast industry. He would have to keep producing hit after hit in order to sustain the needed advertising revenue. And he chose to sell proprietary hardware to users instead of letting them use common tools such as laptops and webcams.

The company ultimately failed, but by starting it, Justin found an even better idea. Justin.tv led to a new app called Socialcam, which allows people to share videos on social media. The app grew to 54.7 million active users a month, and in July 2012, Justin sold it to Autodesk for $60 million.

Justin wrote about the failure of his initial idea:

"It got us started. Some people wait until the stars are aligned before they jump in. Maybe that's the right move, but plenty of businesses get started with something that seems implausible, stupid, or not-a-real-business and turn into something of value. If we hadn't started then, what would we have later?"

Getting started might lead to failure. But what comes from failure can be glorious. It helps you get in the game. It shows you what works and what doesn't. It puts you on the radar of people who matter. And it helps you cross the line from dreamer to doer. Andrew Mason would never have succeeded at Groupon if he had not failed at The Point. Action reveals the path.

In 2003, three students from Helsinki University of Technology started a company that creates mobile games. They didn't have a good idea at first. But they got started and spent the next eight years developing ideas. They created fifty-one games and nearly went bankrupt before finally creating Angry Birds in 2009, which has been downloaded more than two billion times as of this writing and is the most successful mobile game app in history.

Make no mistake—getting started is what's required of you right now. No more theories. No more ideas. No more waiting for the right time or the right set of circumstances. Just start. You'll figure it out later.

Creativity Is a To-Do List

It's bound to happen. We experience something amazing—a great performance, a great meal, or a great book—and we attribute it to magic. Not real magic, of course, but some abstract quality that helps us explain why it's so great and why we could never do it. We assume the artist is larger than life. The chef is a culinary phenomenon. And the writer is once-in-a-lifetime. These experiences seem to transcend our own capabilities, so we pass them off as impossible.

But we couldn't be more wrong. These experiences might appear magical, but they were planned moment by moment, ingredient by ingredient, and page by page. A lot of perspiration went into what we consider to be pure inspiration.

But we don't see it this way. Let me tell you why.

From thirty thousand feet, creativity looks like art. From ground level, it's a to-do list.

In his best-selling book *The E-Myth Revisited*, Michael Gerber describes how he accidentally stumbled upon a hotel on the northern coast of California called Venetia. From the very first moment he stepped into the lobby, his experience was magical. Everything from the outdoor lighting, the soft music, the decor, and the turn-down service to the specific brand of coffee brewing in his room the next morning had been perfectly orchestrated to delight him.

As Michael investigated the reason for his amazing experience that next day in the manager's office, he was presented with a thick three-ring binder labeled Operations Manual. It outlined all of the steps that the hotel employees took to create this magic, including what time the fireplaces were lit and how the staff obtained information about his personal preferences in order to provide a custom experience. In other words, it was all happening because of a to-do list.

> **If people knew how hard I worked to gain my mastery,**
> **it wouldn't seem so wonderful.**
>
> —MICHELANGELO

You and I don't notice the to-do list. We're not supposed to know it exists. But you can't have a perfectly executed, magical experience without one.

Even the Walt Disney Company admits to a less-than-magical formula for success at their theme parks. Here's what their Imagineers wrote in the company treatise *Be Our Guest*: "For the customer, the magic is a source of wonder and enjoyment. For the company and its employees, magic is a much more practical matter."

The overall experience of visiting a Disney park feels like a form of art, but the Imagineers have turned it into a science. They place trashcans no more than twenty-three feet apart (the longest distance someone will carry a piece of garbage); their hotel doors include lower peepholes for kids; and they even change the texture of the pavement from one area of the park to another so that people actually feel when they've entered a new environment.

So much for the magic of Disney.

What we're experiencing is a to-do list. Magical moments require detailed planning, and Disney puts a lot of hard work into it.

Nothing demonstrates the power of a to-do list like the work of an actual magician. When David Copperfield walked through the Great Wall of China on national television in 1986, the overall effect was astounding. With no cutaway shots, David walked up a rolling staircase, entered a cloth box that showed his silhouette, and appeared to walk through the wall.

But what no one noticed amid the suspenseful music and dramatic narration was how David slid into a hidden compartment inside the rolling staircase. Out of the view of cameras and the audience, the staircase was then hoisted over the wall in plenty of time for David to reemerge on the other side. The overall effect was magical, but pulling it off required precise, well-rehearsed steps.

What stops many of us from creating amazing experiences is the misconception that other people are creating magic. We look at their work and say, "I could never do that. They must be special." But in reality, they're just better at creating a to-do list than we are. They have concocted a recipe with all of the right ingredients for success and put them together with focus and hard work.

Your creative vision needs to become a to-do list. List the action steps one by one that make for an amazing experience. And then execute them over and over again until you get it right. It may take days, months, or even years to perfect, but one day, everything will click, and people will say how magical you are.

The Dream Versus the Work of the Dream

Anyone can have a dream. They're easy to come upon. In fact, they come upon us. We have no choice in the matter. We were made to dream. But it's a whole other matter to undertake the work of a dream. This is what keeps many people from achieving their goals. The work of the dream is a barrier to entry.

Here's the difference between a dream and the work of a dream:

Making a list of the people you need to call is the dream.
Picking up the phone and calling them is the work of the dream.

Waiting until you have all the answers is the dream.
Taking steps and learning as you go is the work of the dream.

Telling people you're writing a book is the dream.
Excusing yourself to write in the office is the work of the dream.

Announcing that you're starting an organization is the dream.
Paying an attorney to set up a company is the work of the dream.

Pausing everything to explore a better idea is the dream.
Staying with the first idea until it's done is the work of the dream.

Reading books about leadership is the dream.
Recruiting a team to join you is the work of the dream.

Reading this book is the dream.
Doing something with it is the work of the dream.

There's no question your dream requires hard work. You'll have to work on your dream early in the morning, on weekends, and late at night. You'll be holed up in an office while your friends are having

dinner parties. And you may have to skip the family vacation in order
to afford the start-up costs. But this is the price that dreamers pay.

Achieving your dream is not an exclusive opportunity. There is no
special class of people who get to pursue their dreams while the rest
of us are forced to work at jobs we hate. The entry fee is the same for
everyone, and it's hard work. If you're willing to pay the price, you
can achieve whatever you set out to do.

**Opportunity is missed by most people because it is dressed
in overalls and looks like work.**

— ATTRIBUTED TO THOMAS EDISON

When Will Smith appeared on *The Tavis Smiley Show* in December 2007, he dismissed the idea that his success is due to some special talent. He attributed all of it to hard work:

> *The only thing that I see that is distinctly different about me is
> I'm not afraid to die on a treadmill. I will not be outworked,
> period. You might have more talent than me; you might be
> smarter than me; you might be sexier than me; you might be all
> of those things. You got it on me in nine categories. But if we get
> on the treadmill together, two things: You're getting off first, or
> I'm going to die. It's really that simple.*
>
> *You're not going to outwork me. It's such a simple, basic con-
> cept. The guy who is willing to hustle the most is going to be the
> guy that gets that loose ball. The majority of people who aren't
> getting the places they want or aren't achieving the things that
> they want in this business—it's strictly based on hustle. It's
> strictly based on being outworked. It's strictly based on missing
> crucial opportunities. I say all the time that if you stay ready, you
> ain't gotta get ready.*

If we're not careful, we'll be dreamers all year long without taking one step forward in actual progress. The inertia of dream chasing is to avoid productive activity. In his must-read book *The War of*

Art, Steven Pressfield calls this "the resistance," and it will haunt you at every turn.

The sneaky thing about the resistance is that it doesn't confront you in the forms you would expect, such as writer's block or intimidation. It appears as a valid set of excuses; a setback that justifies quitting; a "no" from someone you were counting on; the feeling that you're not quite ready and need to do more research; a higher-paying job; or a better idea that just came along.

The resistance is convincing. It will make you question your dream. You'll be tempted to put it on the shelf in order to avoid the hard work, rejection, and discomfort. But your dream isn't going anywhere. You will be plagued by your frustration yet again. You can't escape what you were born to do.

Several years ago, a Dream Year participant set out to launch her own business, but the dream overwhelmed her. She kept putting off the work because of her full-time job, a period of sickness, all of the questions that came to mind, friends visiting from out of town, and a number of other reasons. In an attempt to simplify her next step, I boiled down her monthly goal to one single phone call. That's all she needed to do in order to make a significant stride forward—a phone call.

But she never made it.

Another Dream Year participant wanted to open a restaurant, but he couldn't afford to build a permanent location just yet. In his mind, this struck a deathblow to his dream. No matter how much I tried to suggest a catering service or a "pop-up" store in a rented space until the resources became available, he was stalled by the lack of a brick-and-mortar solution to accomplish his dream.

The resistance crushed him.

We use all sorts of excuses to avoid the work of the dream, ranging from "I've got a better idea" to "I'm just too busy right now." We can buy more time by celebrating artificial victories when the actual ones haven't happened. We simply point to an encouraging conversation or cite a new possibility, and we've conveniently stalled our dream for another few months.

Excuses only distract us from the most important work of dreaming—*the doing.* It is the execution—not the perfect set of circumstances or a sufficient amount of money—that brings your dream to life. It is about putting one foot in front of the other until the project is completed.

If you walk only on sunny days, you will never reach your destination.

....

—PAULO COELHO

What will you do to advance your dream? Here are some ideas for how you can keep moving toward the goal of accomplishing your dream:

1. Recognize the time killers in your life and crush them (Twitter, Facebook, video games, Pinterest, Instagram, e-mail, television).
2. Ask this question every morning: "What is the one thing I need to accomplish today?"
3. Form a "collective" that will meet regularly and share the results of their work for the sake of accountability.
4. Find a coach or a mentor to help you stay on course.
5. Set aside blocks of time in your schedule each week as if it were a job.
6. Find the most productive work environment for yourself and show up during scheduled times (office, coffee shop, coworking space).
7. Use a project management system such as Basecamp to complete projects.
8. Break down the project into smaller steps that you can complete.
9. Recruit friends to help or delegate projects to freelancers.
10. Hire a virtual assistant to help you get the work done.

Forget about waiting for better ideas to come along. Forget about generating more ideas. And forget about strategic plans. As former Southwest Airlines CEO Herb Kelleher said, "We have a strategic plan. It's called doing things."

Define Productivity and Do Those Things

The trouble with activity is that it can feel like productivity, even when it accomplishes nothing. Getting your inbox to zero, for example, is not necessarily productive. It makes you feel good. But your e-mail isn't your to-do list. It's other people's to-do list. The key to getting things done is defining what is true productive activity for your dream and doing those things.

If your dream is to write a book, productivity looks like sitting down and actually writing. You can't wait for a good time to write, availability in your schedule, or when inspiration strikes. Your job is to schedule writing sessions on your calendar and show up for work every single time.

If your dream is to sell products, productivity is reaching out to prospective customers. You can't keep tweaking the Web site, postponing phone calls until a better week, or waiting until the marketing materials meet your high standards. You have to reach out to prospects, make appointments, and start selling now. Any other activity won't accomplish your dream.

It's the job never started that takes the longest to finish.

—J.R.R. TOLKIEN

If your dream is to launch an online magazine, a conference, or a retail store, you'll have multiple tasks that fall under true productivity. Make a list of duties and start checking them off. If the task feels too big, break it down into smaller steps. For example, "sell a sponsorship" could become "e-mail their marketing department with a request to discuss the opportunity."

Productivity is not always what you want it to be. Sometimes it's not the work of your craft, but rather finding new clients or raising capital. Sometimes it's things you hate doing, such as managing finances or making a big ask. You'll discover what you hate doing by noticing which things you avoid. Either delegate them or do them. But putting them off is a sure way to stall your dream.

Several years ago, I was the consultant for two businesswomen in Dallas, Stephanie Gardner and Toni Patterson, who were trying to launch a company that connected brides to available wedding venues. They had built an incredible Web site, maintained a thriving Pinterest account, and networked with other bridal services. But so far, they had no revenue. True productivity for them was to meet with venue managers and persuade them to sign a contract to become a part of their network. This way, they could collect a portion of the rental fee from each referral.

When I followed up with them to find out how the business was going, they talked about a new partnership opportunity, updates to the Web site, and some new ideas. But when it came to meeting with venues, they admitted their resistance was winning. I gave them my best locker room speech about the nature of true productivity and challenged them to do the productive work of their dream. Stirred with a newfound passion, they sent promotional mailers to hundreds of venues and followed up with each one by phone. Their business is now enlisting venues and starting to see revenue.

The productive work of your dream is hard. But just because it's hard doesn't mean you shouldn't do it. The "hard" is there to keep *other* people from doing it.

Where Do You Find the Time?

Executing your dream is about making time to get the work done. When you look closely at where your time goes, it's shockingly wasteful. Henry David Thoreau once wrote, "It is not enough to be industrious; so are the ants. What are you industrious about?"

The truth is—you don't have extra time to pursue your dream. No one does. We all wake up to the same number of hours in a day. The only solution is to steal time. We have to remove time from some other endeavor and apply it to our dream. Deciding which endeavor we will sacrifice is painful but necessary.

Best-selling author Anne Lamott once wrote: "I sometimes teach classes on writing during which I tell my students every single thing I know about the craft and habit. This takes approximately 45 minutes. . . . Then I bring up the bad news. You have to make time to do this."

She said her students often point out that they have kids at home, forty-hour workweeks, pets that demand attention, or job searches that take precedence over writing. They insist that they'll eventually do it when their last child moves out or they move to the country or sell their pets.

But Anne says this sort of thinking is delusional. Unless you steal time from something in your life right now, you will never achieve your dream.

Anne suggests swapping out the evening news: "No one needs to watch the news every night, unless one is married to the anchor. Otherwise, you are mostly going to learn more than you need to know about where the local fires are, and how rainy it has been: so rainy!"

She suggests going to the gym fewer times each week; letting your house go without cleaning for longer stretches of time; not volunteering so much; and skipping the frequent carwashes.

I would add skipping NFL football games for a season as well.

In the average televised broadcast of an NFL football game, which lasts 185 minutes, do you know how much of that time is actual play? The answer is eleven minutes.

The Wall Street Journal reported these findings:

Players spend roughly 75 minutes in huddles or milling around at the line of scrimmage. Broadcasters spend 17 minutes showing replays. Cutaway shots to referees and coaches take 13 minutes. Cheerleaders get only 3 seconds of airtime. And commercials can take up to 60 minutes of the broadcast.

In other words, we spend 174 minutes watching pointless activity. Imagine what you could accomplish if you took back that time. Or the time reading up on old girlfriends on Facebook. Or scrolling through your ex-sister-in-law's baby shower photos. Or sleeping in because you watched late-night television.

I love football as much as the next guy, but for eleven minutes of game play, I could skip it for a season and accomplish something productive.

If you still don't think you have the time, try this experiment: Take a week to keep a detailed account of how you spend your time each day, hour by hour. You'll be surprised by the results. Then ask yourself where you could exchange some time for your dream. You may only need a few hours each week. For example, you can write a 48,000-word book in nine months by sitting down three times a week to write 450 words. The question is—what is worth giving up for your dream?

Your Dream Needs a CEO

A Dream Year participant once told me, "My dream is less about who I am than who I need to be." She was right. Dreams require us to become the best version of ourselves.

How many of us cringe at the thought of making a sales call? Or slink out of a room to avoid people rather than walk over to meet them? How many of us keep putting off tasks in favor of excuses? Pursuing a dream exposes how ordinary we are and how fearful we can be.

But not measuring up to the size of our dream is no reason to give up. It's a call to rise up to our potential. How do we do this?

We have to see the dream as its own entity and start acting like its CEO.

What CEO has trouble picking up the phone to make a call? Or what CEO is reluctant to delegate tasks or make a big ask? What CEO can't plan a sales strategy and execute it?

Have you ever met an insecure CEO?

In a society where we're trying to cure multiple personality disorders, your dream is the one place you need it. Your dream requires a clear division of duties between ORDINARY YOU and CEO YOU.

ORDINARY YOU lets the dream get sidetracked by personal issues, time constraints, and emotional drama. Just as the spoiled child of a millionaire can slack off at his parent's business and get away with it, you can take your privileged status as the owner of your dream and slack off without anyone saying a word. No one will challenge you.

But CEO YOU separates your private life from your dream life. She insists that you show up for work. Let me ask you—would your boss let you take off work anytime you felt like it? Would your boss let you get away with unmet deadlines? Probably not. So neither should you.

This is why your dream needs a boss.

ORDINARY YOU is straining to make house payments, pay off car loans, and beat down credit card debt. No wonder you have such low tolerance for risk. When your dream requires capital, ORDINARY YOU looks at the budget and says, "There's no way I can do it."

But CEO YOU strips away the dream from the personal finances and lets it live on its own spreadsheet. This protects the dream from the challenges of your ordinary life. CEO YOU creates a separate financial statement that has nothing to do with ORDINARY YOU's car payment, cable bill, and mortgage and gives the enterprise a chance to live or die by its own revenue and expenses.

When most people pursue a dream, they think they're getting into the activity of their craft (cookie making, magazine editing, event producing, etc.). But what they're *really* getting into is the revenue-seeking side of the business (the sales of cookies, the sales of magazine advertisements, the sales of event tickets). It's the only way the dream can survive. And only a CEO can be objective enough to see this. If you'd rather just do the activity of your craft, it's better to stay employed by someone else.

CEO YOU can only exist if you form an organization around your dream.

Start with the CEO of your dream. Then create the leadership roles in finance, marketing, sales, and operations. It doesn't matter whether you're writing a book or launching a design studio, organize the enterprise of your dream into roles.

Now recruit people to fill each of those roles. They can be volunteer or paid. And if you can't find someone to fill them, write YOUR NAME in each one of those jobs. The point is to hold someone accountable.

Finally, put CEO YOU to work. Your job is to make sure the people in your organization fulfill the work requirements and deadlines of your dream. In other words, YOU need to start cracking the whip on YOU.

We have to strip away the dream from our ordinary selves and let it become an identity in and of itself. We have to protect our dream from the challenges of our personal lives by giving it organization and serving as its CEO. This way, our dream is not being led by a whimsical, insecure, ordinary person.

It is being led by a leader.

The Mind of a Leader

Chasing a dream puts us in charge of our own enterprise. Everything becomes our responsibility. But if we don't have the emotional fortitude to withstand the hard work, pressures, setbacks, and near-brushes with failure, we'll revert back to the mind-set of a hireling:

A hireling values his desires over the good of the organization.

A hireling is committed as long as it's not too hard.

A hireling responds to, rather than initiates, the work of a dream.

A hireling waits to be told what to do.

A hireling believes the business model somehow runs itself.

A hireling sees only her role in the business, not the whole view.

A hireling wants more vacation time at the expense of the work.

A leader, on the other hand, embraces the entire burden of an organization. In the face of difficult pressure or impossible circumstances, a leader stands up to own the moment. He does whatever it takes to see it through.

A hireling goes home.

If you're feeling overwhelmed by the work of your dream or threatened by the circumstances around you, welcome to the role of a leader. What will you do when your dream is at risk of failing? How will you respond when the challenges of life are threatening? In the face of fear, will your response be fight or flight?

Delegate Your Dream

What if you didn't do the work of your dream? What if you walked away from it? I'm not saying you should quit your dream. But what if you weren't the only one who brought your dream to life? What if other people did?

In his best-selling book *The E-Myth Revisited*, Michael Gerber claims that most new businesses fail because their owners are too heavily involved in the activity of the business. Hairdressers choose to cut hair instead of run the shop. Pie makers bake pies instead of working on the overall business.

He goes so far as to say that it would actually be better if you *didn't* know how to do the work of your industry. This way, you'd focus on the overall model of the business and not get lost in the activity of it.

Most of us would never think to pursue a dream of which we had no knowledge. But ignorance can be a great motivator. It forces us to seek out answers and enlist the help of talented people rather than doing it ourselves.

There are great rewards for dreamers who can delegate the work. You get to share the victory with other people. You build camaraderie among friends. You help other people find fulfillment by using their gifts. You get better-quality results by using people more talented than you. And the work doesn't overwhelm you.

I have a friend named Stephanie Beaty who owns a camera. It's the same camera that many other people own. But when she takes photographs, they look different from everyone else's. It's not the tool she uses. It's her eye. It's how she sees through the lens. She captures beautiful moments, and I tell stories about her gift.

Seeing Stephanie's work doesn't make me want to pick up a camera and be like her. It makes me want to *put down* the camera and hire her to shoot photos for me. One look at her work and I quit photography.

Most of us need to do some strategic quitting. We need to abandon the tasks that fall outside of our gifts and focus on the activities of our strengths. We need to find strategic partners who are good at our weaknesses and work with them to produce a better result.

I call this "the bias toward better." We should care so much about the quality of our work that we identify our own weaknesses and fire ourselves from those jobs. There are plenty of talented people who can do it better than we can if we would only ask for help. The greatest expression of our dream depends on it.

As the producer of your dream, it's your job to find people who are better than you are. It's your responsibility to coordinate the efforts of a team to achieve the overall goal. And you have to be able to fire people who aren't working out.

If you're the only one doing all the work, it's really difficult to fire yourself.

It's nepotism at its worst.

There is a point in Dream Year when you should be using the word "we" instead of "me." No matter how talented you are, your dream has a better chance of succeeding with great people around you. It's like being an orchestra conductor. You might be able to play all of the instruments, but why would you want to do that? It's better to direct other talented people.

Your Dream Team

When you set out after your dream, it was a personal decision. It was your idea. It came out of your own passions and interests. It was your baby. So you probably assumed that you had to do this all by yourself.

But nothing could be more destructive to your dream. One person cannot possibly achieve a dream that is truly great. If your dream is a one-person dream, it's not big enough. Great dreams require great teams.

Most likely, you struggle with asking people for help. You can't bring yourself to ask others to work on *your* project. It probably feels selfish to you. It could be fear, insecurity, or lack of confidence or trust, but your dream has become a victim of your own limited capacity.

One of several things is going on here:

- You've come to believe this dream is yours and yours alone. Well, it's not. Your dream is a gift to the world. You don't own it; you are merely a steward of it, and it could have been given to someone else.
- You don't believe that anyone would want to be a part of your dream. This isn't true either. People want to be a part of great things. They just don't know how to get involved. You have to ask them.
- You don't trust other people to execute with excellence. You've been burned before. If this has happened to you, resolve to build trust and work with better people. Be a relentless recruiter of great talent.

Several years ago, I wanted to work with graphic designer Gary Dorsey of Pixel Peach Studio in Austin, Texas. I've always loved his imaginative designs, but he wouldn't return my e-mails. And he didn't need to return them. His client roster is a who's who of celebrities and musicians. But I kept e-mailing him every few months, carrying on a one-sided conversation, as if he might be interested in my projects.

Two years later, on a flight to Chicago, I resolved to e-mail him one last time. It seemed futile, but I sent him a link to my Flickr page, which featured the latest photos from my STORY conference.

I figured that was the end of that.

To my surprise, I got an e-mail from Gary the next day, expressing his admiration for the event. He said he wanted to help create the branding for the next one. When we caught up over the phone, price wasn't even an issue for him. He had been sold on the vision, and we have been working together ever since.

Invite other people to join your dream. Be up front about whether you can afford to pay them or whether you're looking for volunteers. But cast vision for the greater purpose of your dream, not just the tasks. In other words, share why you're doing it. What great problem are you solving in the world? People will join you because they want to be a part of something great, not because they're looking for a payoff.

The iconic businessman Sam Walton used to say, "Capital isn't scarce. Vision is." I would add that great teams aren't scarce. Vision is.

Here are some ways to find people to help with your dream:

1. Dream big. Great dreams attract great people.
2. Create exceptional branding. Great ideas have great brands.
3. Host vision meetings where people can join a community.
4. Ask people for a commitment. They want to be asked.
5. Give others credit for the success and take responsibility for failure.
6. Provide role descriptions. People want to know what's expected of them.
7. Believe in them. When you trust people, they come through.
8. Celebrate wins as a team. It will attract other people.

Great Groups

Leadership guru Warren Bennis wrote in his book *Organizing Genius* that great dreams are brought to life by teams of talented people who come together for a short season and pour themselves into the work. These "great groups" have a few characteristics:

- They're made up of gifted people.
- They're engaged in creating something new.
- They have no trouble keeping up morale.
- Money doesn't matter to them.
- The quality of the work space doesn't matter either.
- They tend to have a playful, adolescent subculture.
- They have confidence to overcome the impossible.
- They're led by extraordinary leaders.
- They often fall apart when the project is completed.

Michelangelo wasn't a solitary artist. He surrounded himself with a cohort of artists who produced other great works. In fact, thirteen of them helped him paint the ceiling of the Sistine Chapel.

In the 1940s, Henrietta Mears, the education director at First Presbyterian Church of Hollywood, California, taught a class that produced hundreds of ministry leaders. Three of them gathered around her breakfast table on a regular basis. You might know them as evangelist Billy Graham, Dawson Trotman, who founded The Navigators, and Bill Bright, who started Campus Crusade for Christ.

Around the same time, a group of scholars and writers gathered at The Eagle and Child pub in Oxford, England, to discuss theology and literature. Among this group were C. S. Lewis, J.R.R. Tolkien, Owen Barfield, and Charles Williams. Calling themselves the Inklings, they produced some of the greatest works in Christian literature.

In 1992, Bill Clinton assembled a world-class team to run his presidential campaign, including speechwriter Paul Begala, his wife

Hillary Rodham Clinton, fund-raiser Rahm Emanuel, strategist James Carville, and communications director George Stephanopoulos. Together, they operated out of "The War Room" to resurrect Clinton's impossible bid for the presidency after it was rocked by the scandal of Gennifer Flowers's allegations that they'd had an affair.

Bill Gates became fast friends with Paul Allen at a very young age and eventually they started Microsoft together. Steve Jobs met Steve Wozniak when they were teenagers and they stayed friends to launch Apple. Both of these start-ups attracted thousands of exceptional people who gave significant portions of their lives to bring a great vision to life.

The list of great groups goes on and on. But the important question is this—whom are you inviting to help bring your dream to life? Where is your great group? Take the organizational chart you composed in this chapter and begin writing in the names of people who would be well suited for the roles. You may not be able to pay them right now, but start casting vision for accomplishing a great dream together.

Call to Action

There would be no greater tragedy than to go through all of life as a dreamer but to have never taken a single step toward your dream. Dreaming is the easy part. Anyone can do that. This year is about execution. It's time to fire "ordinary you" and put "CEO you" in charge. If you're not up to the task, remember this—Dream Year is less about who you are than who you need to become. If you're the same person one year from now that you are today, you haven't done it right.

There's only one thing that can get you through the difficulty of bringing a dream to life—a schedule. Set aside a time each day or each week when you'll sit down to do the hard work. And then show up each and every time. Put it on your calendar. Don't schedule things on top of it. Refuse to let friends sabotage it with other plans.

If they ask, you're simply "not available." Make it your job and show up for work.

So this is it. No more excuses. No more distractions. Set a schedule. Write it below. Put it on your calendar. Show up for work and stick to it.

QUESTIONS:

1. Pursuing a dream is more about who you need to become than who you are. What activities are waiting for "CEO you" to start tackling?

2. To achieve your dream, you must become an architect of a vision-producing system. This can be a schedule, an outline, or a to-do list. But what system do you need to create to complete the work? Create it this week.

3. Great dreams require great teams. What people come to mind when you think about a "dream team"? Start having conversations with them.

THE BIG ASK

After the final no there comes a yes
And on that yes the future world depends.

—WALLACE STEVENS, "THE WELL DRESSED MAN WITH A BEARD"

You Can't Be a Dream Chaser
Without Being a Rainmaker

The minute you started pursuing your dream, you took on the role of a rainmaker. A rainmaker is someone who brings in revenue. And if you are running the endeavor that is your dream, you cannot deflect or delegate this responsibility.

Most people go to their jobs each day oblivious to the economic engine that is their company. They show up for work, complete their responsibilities, and then get paid for it. They have no regard for the profit and loss statement.

But the most conscientious employees know exactly how much they're contributing to their organizations. They understand whether they're adding to the revenue stream or taking resources from it. This is why personal assistants and project managers often get laid off before the sales team in an economic downturn. It's hard to say goodbye to the rainmakers.

I've resolved that if I ever work for another company again, I want to be on the revenue-producing side of the balance sheet. I want to contribute at least two, three, and four times my paycheck.

In the case of Apple stores, the average employee helps generate about $420,000 of annual sales for the company each year.

Being a rainmaker comes with better job security.

The same goes for your dream. It will never come to life unless you bring in the revenue to sustain it. Dreaming can be expensive.

I once spoke with the young founder of a social justice organization that cares for orphans and victims of sex trafficking in Africa. It's a remarkable organization, but he was frustrated, even angry, at the costs of carrying out his mission. When I asked him whether he'd approached anyone for donations lately, he said, "I'm good at communicating and caring for people, but fund-raising is hard for me."

I told him what I'm telling you now. If you're going to chase your dream, you have to take on the responsibility of generating revenue. You can't be a dream chaser without being a rainmaker. Otherwise, you'll always be hurting for money.

After my compassionate friend and I worked through all of the alternatives to raising money—working another job, selling his possessions, helping fewer people—my friend determined with great clarity, "I need to start making asks or I need to stop doing this."

It all comes down to making asks.

Making Asks

Rainmakers generate revenue by making asks. They ask for donations. They ask for contracts. They ask for deals. They ask for opportunities. They ask to meet with leaders or speak to them over the phone. They ask for publicity. They come up with ideas and ask for a few minutes of your time to pitch it. They ask for help.

Don't let rainmaking deter you from your dream. It's one of the barriers to entry, and you can overcome it. Once you taste the sweet victory of a positive response, you'll not only become comfortable with it, you might even enjoy it. But making asks is the only way to bring your dream to life.

Asking is a lot easier to do when you've paved the way for it.

Make friends first and sales later. It pays to get to know other people and build trust for the moment you need it. Many of us are guilty of making the "too early ask" where we haven't built up enough social capital beforehand. But if you have no other choice and cold calling is your only option, ask anyway. You never know what might come of it.

Bob Goff is an attorney and the founder of Restore International, an organization that seeks justice for the atrocities committed against children, such as slavery, sexual abuse, and even mutilation. On September 11, 2001, when hijacked planes slammed into the World Trade Towers, Bob came home from work to break the news to his young children around the breakfast table. To help them process the tragedy, he asked them what they would say to a group of world leaders if they had the chance.

His daughter had the audacious idea to write letters to these presidents, prime ministers, and rulers to ask for a personal meeting with them. Not one to stifle his daughter's imagination, Bob obliged her by retrieving the leaders' names and addresses from the CIA Web site and setting up a post office box to avoid giving out his family's home address. He didn't believe any of them would actually respond.

To Bob's amazement, the replies started coming back. The leaders who declined the offer were cordial. Some even handwrote their responses, including Great Britain's Tony Blair. But finally, they started receiving acceptances. Countries such as Bulgaria, Switzerland, and Israel invited the children to come and meet with their leaders. In all, they received twenty-nine positive responses. And Bob took his kids to every one of these meetings.

Life shrinks or expands according to one's courage.

—ANAÏS NIN

All of this happened because of a simple ask.

I have appointed myself the chief rainmaker of my dreams. I have funded every new organization and project I've ever started by making ask after ask. And because of this, I've been rejected over and over again. I probably receive twenty rejections for every positive response I get. So when one of my projects launches, you are looking at the fruit of a series of asks. Enough people have said yes.

If you're struggling financially right now, it's not because you have a money problem. It's because you have an "ask problem." Whatever fear, insecurity, or intimidation is holding you back, determine that it will stop you no longer. As Oprah Winfrey said, "You get in life what you have the courage to ask for."

The Art of the Ask

There are certain "asks" I hate to make. I hate asking people to help me move. I hate asking friends to watch our kids. And I hate asking clients to pay early for the sake of my cash flow. But asking people to be a part of my dream is not one of them. I believe in what I'm asking. I believe in the life-giving benefits of participating in a dream.

When it's hard for me to make the "ask," it's either because I'm insecure or I don't really believe in what I'm doing. Failure to ask can be a sign of unbelief. Plenty of ideas make it out of the boardroom of your mind but falter in the streets of action. You know how badly you want something by how much you're willing to ask for it.

Reluctance can also be a matter of motive. If you're trying to take advantage of someone, then of course asking is going to be difficult—unless you're a scoundrel. But if you're realizing your dream by also fulfilling someone else's desires, you're giving value to that person. This is a request you can be proud to make. You're not asking them to do what *you* want. You're asking them to do what *they* want. You are framing your ask around a dream of their own. By combining your interests into one collaborative endeavor, you're creating a win-win scenario.

While working for a company years ago, I was responsible for developing a continuity membership program that offered exclusive content, access to a special community, and quarterly resources in the mail. When I noticed how many publishers were clamoring to provide free books to our audience of young leaders, I put together a program that would accomplish both of our goals.

I asked publishers for $10,000 to include one book in each of our quarterly mailings, which were sent to two thousand people. It might seem absurd that they would give away eight thousand books *and* pay us $10,000. But putting their books in the hands of young leaders was important to them. They would have had to pay the shipping costs anyway. So the publishers got their books in the right hands. Our audience got great resources. And we made a profit from the program. Everyone walked away happy.

You can feel guilty for making asks, or you can see the value it brings to other people and swing away. This is the challenge of a rainmaker—to view your dream through the eyes of other people.

If you don't have direct access to the person you want to approach, ask a mutual friend to connect you, introduce yourself at a conference, reach out on Twitter, send a message on LinkedIn, call their company's switchboard and ask for their office, or even guess their e-mail address by trying multiple combinations of their name at their Web address one at a time until the e-mails stop bouncing back.

I once secured a partnership with a popular hotel chain by spotting the name of its senior vice president in *Fast Company*. I guessed his e-mail address by trying multiple combinations of his first and last name at the parent company's Web address. Both of my e-mails went unreturned, but he instructed the head of partnerships to contact me. I proposed a partnership based on the fact that our conference attendees book hundreds of hotel nights, often selling out an entire property. Not only this, but our audience reflects the same kind of consumers they're trying to reach. I framed the ask on what our event could do for their brand, not what we wanted from the deal.

Your first ask should be for a phone call. Make it easy to say yes to a first small step. Give them a chance to get to know you before you pitch a bigger plan. Identify what's important to them and let them know you've got an idea to support it. A publisher wants to sell books. A hotel chain wants to fill rooms. A record label wants to sell albums. And a nonprofit wants more donors. Start with what matters to them and then look for how your proposition serves their interests.

When my filmmaker friend Kristin Harle wanted to secure the film rights to one of her favorite childhood books, she explained to the Iowa-based publisher that a film would help them sell more books. They put her in touch with the author to begin conversations. And when Dream Year participant and fashion designer Jenna Quintana wanted to sell her dresses in a Portland, Oregon, clothing store, she appealed to the store owner's desire to mentor a young woman by asking for advice on how to make it in fashion. The owner didn't just agree to meet with her; she took her to lunch. This was Jenna's first step in getting the owner to consider carrying her line.

Asking people to contribute to your dream—whether it's money, time, or talent—is an act of generosity. You're inviting them to participate with you in a dream that is greater than the sum of its parts. Many people don't go after great dreams, so the world is in awe of those who do. They're thrilled to be a part of what you're doing.

Never Say No for Other People

It's tragic how we become paralyzed by the fear of rejection. Before we take one step toward our dream—before we even try to see what's possible—we quit because we don't want to be turned away.

In his best-selling book *The 4-Hour Work Week*, Timothy Ferriss describes how he challenged a Princeton University class to make personal contact with a seemingly impossible person to reach, such as Bill Clinton, J.Lo, or J. D. Salinger. The first student to do so would win a round-trip ticket to anywhere in the world.

Timothy was prepared to pay for the trip. In fact, the rules were such that anyone could have turned in a one-paragraph response and collected the prize. But no one even attempted the experiment. Timothy explained that the students didn't believe they could beat their classmates, so they gave up without trying.

Here's an important lesson.

Never say no for other people.

That's their job.

In the pursuit of your dream, everyone has a job. Your job is to dream audaciously, act courageously, and make big asks. *Their* job is to say yes or no. And this is their job and their job alone.

Life begins at the end of your comfort zone.

—NEALE DONALD WALSCH

Babe Ruth is known as the home run king of baseball. He was the first player to hit sixty home runs in one season. Some say baseball became popular only when he started playing. When you think of Babe Ruth, you don't think of failure. But get this—from 1926 until 1964, Babe Ruth held Major League Baseball's career *strikeout record.*

The thing that brought success to his career was the very thing that brought failure. He swung at a lot of pitches, and most of them never connected.

Rejection clears the playing field. If you can handle rejection, you'll become part of a small fraternity of dreamers who see their ideas become a reality. When you make it past the first few rejections, the field of competitors begins to thin out.

We have got to be people who are at ease with rejection. There is a "yes" waiting for us out there, and the only way to find it is by sifting through all of the "nos."

One of Dream Year's participants, Justin Wise, wanted to attend financial guru Dave Ramsey's EntreLeadership event in April 2008. This exclusive conference hosts just 150 people in a prestigious location at a price tag of $4,000.

Justin couldn't afford to go, but he believed there was a yes waiting for him, so he decided to make a big ask. He sent Dave an e-mail expressing his desire to attend but explained that he couldn't afford it. He asked if he could attend for free. Justin didn't know if Dave would even get the e-mail. But one week later, he received a surprising response. Not only did Dave send a personal invitation to be his guest, but he also paid for Justin's airfare and hotel room.

I wonder how many of us in Justin's position would have said no for Dave before ever writing that e-mail.

As we go about making asks, some doors will open and others will close. But we have to persevere in the asking. We have to keep trying doorknobs. Because when we press through rejection, when we sift through all of the "nos," something remarkable happens. We eventually find a "yes," and our dream comes one step closer to reality.

They're Not Opposed, Just Busy

Our problem is not that we fear rejection. Rejection is worth fearing. Who likes being turned down? Our problem is that we reject ourselves. We assume that people don't want to hear from us, so we don't reach out. We're pessimists about ourselves. So we give up without trying. We reject our own ideas long before anyone else does.

How tragic.

How unfounded.

How unnecessary.

I once worked for an executive who continually pushed me to make asks. One day, I told him that contacting people who didn't return my calls or e-mails felt like harassment. If they were interested, they would call me back, I reasoned.

He swiveled around in his chair and said, "Ben, people are busy. Yours is not the only e-mail or phone call they're getting. At the moment when you think you're harassing them, they're just starting to notice you. Don't just assume that they're not interested in hearing from you."

I decided to take his word for it. So every time I felt reluctant to make another call, I reminded myself of what he said and pushed through. Every time I thought all hope was lost, I tried one more time. And do you know—it worked! Without fail, that one additional call or e-mail garnered a response that went something like this:

"Ben, I'm so sorry for not getting back to you. We just finished up a big project, and I'm finally going through my e-mails. I'd love to set up an appointment to talk."

Do you know how good it feels to get that kind of response after a long series of failed connections? It's enough to restore your faith in your dream. It wasn't that they were uninterested. I just wasn't persistent.

This was the start of a new mantra for my professional life: People aren't opposed. They're just busy.

You must do the thing you think you cannot do.

—ELEANOR ROOSEVELT

How can you tell the difference between someone who is avoiding you, as opposed to just busy? The last thing you want to be is the bane of someone's existence. Here are some ways to persevere without ruining relationships:

1. Give them plenty of time to respond. Wait a week before following up.
2. When you do contact them again, try a different method—e-mail, text, call, or Twitter. Some people are not "e-mail people." They're "text people" or "phone call people." Find their preferred method.
3. Be brief in your correspondence. Say it "above the fold." No scrolling or PDF attachments in the first e-mail.
4. Give them one easy thing to respond to. Do all the work for them. Make it easy to say yes to the next small step.
5. If they say "no," "that's not for me," or any other cue, respect them with a kind word and by all means, stop asking.
6. If they decline the first ask, all is not lost with the relationship. Don't be afraid to come back later with a different ask.

7. Be courteous and considerate in all of your communications. How you respond to rejection will help you or hurt you when you come back later. Make a good impression that you can build on.
8. Don't let your emotions get the best of you. Give them the benefit of the doubt. Don't give up until they actually tell you "no."

Why We Get Rejected

Our dreams are not just about the destination. They're about the journey. There is a reason we get rejected, and it's meant to serve a bigger purpose. There are three possible things going on here:

1. There's a better way.

You can either look at your rejected request as "Plan A" that bombed or as "Plan B" that was undertaken in the wrong order. So pick yourself up. Dust yourself off. And go after the better thing. It's out there. It's always been out there. You just knocked on the neighbor's door by mistake.

2. You're developing thick skin.

What if your dream required strong emotional fortitude and you didn't have it yet? Would you allow your circumstances to shape you? Unfortunately, we can't develop thick skin by resolving to have it. We get it by being rejected over and over again. Eventually, it stops fazing us.

3. It's keeping other people from achieving your dream.

Think of rejection as a barrier to entry. If all you got were easy "yeses," then anyone could go after your dream and achieve it. Then what would you do? Your perseverance is what sets you apart. Those "nos" make your dream a treasure.

The interesting thing about rejection is that we fear it far more than it deserves to be feared. I hate the idea of getting flu shots at the doctor, but they hurt much less than I imagine. I hate the idea of losing money on a business venture, but I can recover from it more easily than I think.

> **Most of the important things in the world have been accomplished by people who have kept on trying when there seemed to be no hope at all.**
>
> —DALE CARNEGIE

Stepping out to pursue your dream is risky. You'll feel anxious, stressed out, fearful, and desperate at times. But desperation is a powerful motivator. It feels awful, but it can be a force for good. There's nothing like desperation to disrupt your comfort and compel you to make asks. Without this pressure, it's much more difficult to send e-mails and make calls to people who intimidate you.

Sure, you can avoid rejection by not trying at all. But you'll have absolutely no shot at greatness either. This is your calling—to face your fears, surrender your comfort, and live life to the fullest no matter how challenging it can be. It's worth it.

Nike once aired a commercial featuring this confession from basketball legend Michael Jordan:

I've missed more than nine thousand shots in my career.
I've lost almost three hundred games.
Twenty-six times I've been trusted to take the game-winning shot . . . and missed.
I've failed over and over and over again in my life.
And that is why I succeed.

It's Not Who You Know. It's Who They Know

Your dream comes to life through other people.

In 2007, I got an e-mail from a creative director in Florida named Stephen Brewster. He had been reading my blog and reached out to make a personal connection. We had an instant rapport, and over the next year, it grew into a genuine friendship. Little did I know that his friendship was going to catapult a dream of mine into existence.

I had transitioned into a new job running events for a company in Atlanta, and Stephen got hired as the senior director of marketing for a major music label. I was tasked with launching a new conference on the West Coast and needed a larger-than-life band to put it on the map. I had no budget to afford them, but the band I wanted happened to be on Stephen's label.

It was an audacious ask. But that's what friends are for, right?

I had barely gotten the question out before Stephen said he was on it. Without an ounce of reservation, he called the label's vice president of A&R, who was a close friend of his and a mentor to the band, and presented our case. He cast vision for the conference, explained why it was a great opportunity, and suggested ways to pay for the band's trip to California. I think he may have put his job on the line.

But it worked.

Stephen helped me bring Hillsong United to the event for nothing but the cost of their hotel rooms. Normally this would have been a $125,000 expense, but their whole band traveled from Sydney, Australia, to perform on the music label's dime. Stephen explained it was a great opportunity to play in a new market for an influential young audience. But mostly, the band trusted his recommendation. They used the trip to play a few more shows on the West Coast, Stephen's label sold a lot of albums, our attendees were elated, and everybody won.

Friendship is the conduit for your dream's success. You have to be a maker of friends. Otherwise you'll never have the courage to make important asks.

What happens if you don't have friends in high places? What if they're not connected or influential or willing to help?

Please read this very carefully:

It's not who *you* know; it's who *they* know.

Sometimes the best thing your friend will ever do for you is to introduce you to someone else. In fact, most of my dreams haven't come about because of my own friends, but because of the people they knew.

Have you ever heard of "six degrees of separation"? It says that everyone is, at most, six connections away from any other person in the world. But I believe it's even closer when it comes to your dream. You are only one or two steps away from the right person to help your dream succeed.

In 2010, Mark Clement joined Dream Year to create a short film that would help him move out of making corporate videos for a living and into feature films. As we discussed helpful connections in our coaching sessions, Mark realized that he was just one person away from the following people:

Tony Hale, an actor on TV's *Arrested Development*

William Paul Young, author of the best-selling novel *The Shack*

Rob Venditti, author of the graphic-novel-turned-movie *The Surrogates*

Max Handelman, movie producer of *The Surrogates*

A billionaire investor who already had a passion for making movies

Mark lives in Birmingham, Alabama, which is a long way from Hollywood. But he discovered the power of friends in just one degree of separation.

Oftentimes, your friends are in a better position to make an ask than you are. People base their decisions on the asker, not the ask. If they don't know who you are, why should they say yes? You need the right "asker," and it might not be you.

In 2011, I wanted to recruit a popular actor to speak at STORY, but I didn't have any personal connections to Hollywood. I began surveying my friends, looking for relationships, when I remembered that my good friend Bethany worked at the International Justice Mission in Washington, D.C. IJM is a human rights organization that rescues victims of violence, sexual exploitation, slavery, and oppression. Knowing that notable causes often attract celebrity advocates, I called Bethany to see if our conference could bring awareness to IJM's efforts around the world in exchange for leveraging one of these influential relationships for a keynote address.

Bethany remembered that the actor Sean Astin from *The Lord of the Rings*, *The Goonies*, and *Rudy* once attended a presentation by IJM's founder Gary Haugen and felt moved to be a part of it. She made no promises but said she would reach out to a friend who knew Sean personally to make an ask on our behalf.

It took a few months to get an answer. In fact, we purchased Sean's airline ticket without a firm commitment because the date was getting so close. But eventually Sean said yes and we introduced him to a standing ovation at the event. Not only did he have a great time and our audience loved it, but Bethany gave a powerful presentation about IJM's work in freeing slaves, which led to a $90,000 donation from one of our attendees' organizations.

Finding the right asker can make all the difference.

Desperation is sometimes as powerful an inspirer as genius.

—BENJAMIN DISRAELI

In 2012, I was preparing to invite best-selling author Anne Lamott to speak at STORY for the third time after two failed attempts. Both times, either my proposed fee was too low or she was too busy. And her agent, a lovely person, was firm about not pushing too hard.

One day, I saw Anne tweet about another author who happened to speak at STORY a few years prior. It dawned on me that I was the wrong person to be making the ask. I reached out to the author and asked if he would make a recommendation on our behalf. He agreed and told me to contact her agent again the next day. When I put in the formal request, Anne agreed right away. The agent remarked that she'd never seen Anne respond so quickly to an invitation.

Good relationships are the key to bringing dreams to life. Here is how you can cultivate friendships and pave the way for future asks:

1. Respond to every e-mail and phone call. Say no if you must, but always be courteous and kind. You never know who people might turn out to be.
2. Listen carefully for who your friends know, what connections they have, or where they've worked in the past.
3. Never underestimate the power of social media in making helpful connections.
4. Make your needs known. Your colleagues and friends can't help you if you don't mention what you need.
5. If you host planning meetings or brainstorming gatherings, invite your friends to bring their friends and expand your connections.
6. Reach out to people you don't know. Every friendship begins as a first encounter.
7. Schedule time in your day to make new connections, even just twenty minutes.
8. Take initiative in reaching out to people in your industry. Maybe they know about you but are waiting for you to make the first move.
9. Host parties, meet-ups, and luncheons. Maybe you're more comfortable in groups than one-on-one.
10. Or try one-on-one meetings. Find the best way for you to connect.

Call to Action

Rainmaking is unfamiliar territory for those who have been clueless about the economic engines of their employers. But as a dream chaser, only you will be concerned about creating revenue and opportunities for your endeavor. It all comes down to making asks. At first, this is an uncomfortable undertaking. But the more you do it, the easier it gets and the more at ease you become with rejection.

And you're going to get rejected a lot.

But don't lose heart. Like the strikeout king Babe Ruth, when you swing at a lot of pitches, some of them will connect with the ball and clear the fences. The very thing that brings rejection is the very thing that will bring success. Your only job is to make the ask. Don't talk yourself out of it. Don't assume what others will say. And by all means, never say no for other people. That's their job and their job alone.

Make a list of the people you need to approach and the asks you need to make in order to bring your dream to life. You'll be tempted to scratch people off the list. You'll want to remove some asks because they feel too big. But don't you dare give up before you do it.

Dream Year is about making the big ask.

QUESTIONS:

1. On a scale of 1 to 10, how comfortable are you with the role of rainmaker? Are you willing to be rejected if it means growing thicker skin and getting closer to finding a "yes"?
2. How can you become a better maker of friends? In other words, how can you build stronger friendships before you make asks?
3. Who have you given up on because they didn't respond right away? What if they weren't opposed, but just busy?

BRANDING YOUR DREAM

Design is not just what it looks like and feels like.
Design is how it works.
....
—STEVE JOBS

Designing the Experience

It's not enough to merely offer a product, a service, or a cause to the world. That works fine for flea markets and yard sales. But when it comes to your dream, people want a compelling experience they can't get anywhere else.

This experience is your brand.

It includes graphic design, but it's so much more than that. It's the feeling, personality, language, style, and overall approach of your dream.

It's the way you come at the world.

It can be all-encompassing like the handbook for a Ritz-Carlton or as simple as the checkerboard décor and hamburger menu of a Five Guys restaurant. But if you don't decide what this experience will be, every good idea will steer you in a different direction, and the results won't be pretty.

Branding is tantamount to caring about your dream and the people you serve. It includes how you answer the phone, the paper stock of your business cards, the colors in your logo, and the look of your videos. If you do it right, the experience becomes greater than the sum of its parts. It makes you better than you actually are.

Here are several brand experiences I enjoy:

- Valentine Freeman curates the blog for Ace Hotels, which is an outlet for the brand's progressive, street-smart personality. Valentine is entrusted with understanding and championing this spirit for Ace. She said, "Content has to catch the right glimmer of light for me. If it feels off, or like it compromises who we are, I decline it or find ways to bring it closer to home."

- I'm not a big fan of country knickknacks in my own home, but I can't resist the down-home charm of a Cracker Barrel restaurant. Every restaurant features the same general store, country menu, wooden latticework, and rocking chairs outside. No store deviates from this proven formula. It's all I can do not to pick up a Gatlin Brothers CD in the gift shop.

- Malcolm Gladwell has written five books and all of them appear to be a part of the same series. The covers feature the same white background, a similar typeface for the title, and a single object that represents the book's theme. Malcolm's branding extends across all of his books and his Web site, which creates a thoughtful, intellectual impression on readers.

- Longman & Eagle is a charming gastro pub in Chicago that offers six rooms for rent upstairs in a small boutique hotel. None of the rooms go for the same price, just as none of the chairs in the dining room match. There are more than forty whiskeys on the menu, some of which complement nothing. It might seem random, but every element is curated to achieve an eclectic style.

- Every catalog for Urban Outfitters makes me wish I could relive my twenties, taking pictures of my beautiful friends at sunset, sifting through rock-and-roll albums at the local music store, and lugging a canoe over my head through the city streets for some strange reason—all while wearing fashionable clothing. The company's goal is to create an emotional bond with customers between the ages of eighteen and thirty.

Organizations that create remarkable brands are intentional about how they're perceived by the world. If you don't have a vision for what this experience will be, you'll be tossed and turned by every whim and fancy.

This is how graffiti gets started in public restrooms. Someone in the chain of command decided it didn't matter anymore. That is, of course, unless they wanted it to be a part of the brand.

The grocery industry used to be cluttered with the same utilitarian warehouse stores where every Dick, Jane, and Harry shopped for their weekly necessities. But then Whole Foods decided to start caring about the grocery business and turned food shopping into a unique experience.

They target the same upscale customers that stores like Neiman Marcus go after. But rather than touting a stuffy affluence, they make it accessible to everyone. Sure, they charge $15 for sandwiches at the deli counter, but they make the experience more personal by posting signs that announce who sliced the meats that day and what kind of cheeses go with them.

The employees aren't there purely for customer service. They roam the aisles, engaging customers as if they're genuinely happy to be there. You're not only invited to shop in the store but also to enjoy some coffee or bring your family for dinner. It's a refreshing twist to an otherwise monotonous experience.

Create your own visual style. Let it be unique for yourself and yet identifiable for others.

—ORSON WELLES

Designing a brand is about creating more than a transaction. You're creating unique moments. You're setting yourself apart from everyone else who tries to do what you do. And you're paying respect to the customers who make it all possible by giving them something of the utmost quality and value.

A well-designed brand creates an emotional experience for people. Just as a screenwriter tries to make you cry or laugh in a movie, your job is to evoke an emotional experience from people who encounter your dream. And that includes you. Being proud of your brand makes you more confident to offer it to the world.

The Story Behind Your Brand

Branding is much easier when there's a story behind the experience. People don't want transactions. They want a narrative that is more exciting than their own lives.

They want to feel like they're eating croissants at an actual French bakery, even if they *are* sitting in a suburban strip mall in the Midwest. When mothers buy orange juice for their kids, they want to believe it just came off the farmer's truck. And don't mess with someone wearing a TapouT shirt because they might actually believe they're an Ultimate Fighter.

Amusement parks invent stories around rides to make the experience more compelling. Verbolten at Busch Gardens in Williamsburg, Virginia, is a journey through the forbidden Black Forest in Germany. The Jaws ride at Universal Studios in Hollywood turns you into a resident of the fictional town of Amity so you can experience the horror of a shark attack. And Harry Potter and the Forbidden Journey in Orlando takes people for a ride on an "enchanted bench" through the halls of Hogwarts, into the Forbidden Forest, and onto the playing fields for a Quidditch match. Without these stories, let's face it: you're just getting water splashed in your face and jerked around on metal tracks.

The same is true for your dream. People want a story. It can be true or made up, but the one with the best story wins.

Dos Equis turned its beer into an international success by creating a story line about "The Most Interesting Man in the World." Its ads feature the elderly but debonair actor Jonathan Goldsmith performing all sorts of superhuman and interesting feats. Dos Equis's senior brand director Paul Smailes said he chose an older man so that younger men would not "see him as a threat or as a reminder of accomplishments they hadn't achieved yet." The story helped grow the brand's sales by 22 percent at a time when other craft beers dropped 4 percent.

Dos Equis used an outlandish fable to sell its product. You'll find similar tactics from The Kraken rum, whose ads feature a legendary sea creature, and Jameson Irish whiskey, whose namesake John Jameson goes to great lengths to recover his alcohol from villains. But your story could be as simple as how your company got its name, or the process by which you manufacture products. Our maker society values knowing how and why you do what you do. It's imperative that you tell your story.

Having a story doesn't mean you tell it all the time or even to everyone. But it gives your dream a sense of context to help shape your brand's experience.

Here are some questions to ask as you craft your own story:

1. Why did you get started with your dream? What was the "great need" that compelled you to pursue it?
2. How did you get started? What were the circumstances around your beginning? How can you create a legend out of it?
3. What characters are important to your brand? Are you the only one as the founder or was your dream inspired by a relative or another person?
4. What antagonists or enemies does your dream have? They don't have to be actual people. They can be "mundane family meals" or the threat of your secret family recipe getting out. But great stories have a nemesis.
5. How does this story translate into other aspects of your offering, such as the Web site, the design, and your promotions?

Naming Things

A great brand starts with a great name. It can be a made-up name like Twitter; a combination of words like GrubHub; a repurposed word like Uber; or even a new way of thinking about words, such as Airbnb and Dwolla. But your name will make or break you. Choose the right one, and it will attract people. Choose the wrong one and it will confuse or even deter them.

Bryan Allain from Lancaster, Pennsylvania, joined Dream Year in 2011 to launch an organization that helps people build online communities. Bryan is a successful blogger with a substantial following, so he wanted to share his insights with other people. He initially called it "Blog Rocket," but there was a problem with the name. Blogs are being overtaken by more socially driven sites, such as Twitter, Pinterest, Facebook, and Instagram. By catering only to bloggers, he was missing an opportunity to connect with a much larger audience of social media users.

Bryan struggled with renaming something he had already started until, several weeks later, he received an unsolicited offer from another company to buy his domain. Bryan couldn't pass up the offer. He sold the name, changed his brand to Killer Tribes, which includes all social media platforms, and expanded his offerings to conferences, classes, books, and communities.

Here are several ways to choose a name for your dream. Keep in mind this doesn't cover every approach. You'll have to find the strategy that works for you.

1. List all of the possibilities.

Our tendency is to pick a favorite early on and stick with it through the entire process. But fight the temptation. The brand consultancy Interbrand came up with more than a thousand names for Microsoft's search engine before settling on "Bing."

2. Find strong associations.

Scott Frigaard of Fairfax, Virginia, launched a security company that provides online surveillance for municipalities. He wanted a name that invoked strength, security, and virtual monitoring. After numerous naming sessions, he came up with Iron Sky, which accomplishes all of these objectives.

Strong associations practically sell your product for you. Think about the name "Krispy Kreme." It uses two contradictory but delightful concepts to describe their sweet pastries. Elsie Larson from Springfield, Missouri, called her popular lifestyle blog "A Beautiful Mess," which sounds contradictory but creates an alluring concept that reflects her eclectic approach to fashion, food, crafts, and photography.

3. Build the meaning into the name.

Be careful not to choose a name that's so unique it requires an explanation. If you can interchange your dream's name for any industry, any film, any book, any product, or any company, you may have to do a lot of explaining until people catch on. "Groupon" combines the words "group" and "coupon" to explain what they do, and "Sport Clips" appeals to guys who want to get their hair trimmed while watching games on TV. You can be unique without being cryptic.

4. Get feedback from other people.

One of the participants of Dream Year 2010, Kendra Malloy, wanted to come up with the perfect name for her online travel service. She surveyed more than 120 friends on Facebook with six possibilities—one was her top choice, two were runners-up, and three were throwaways. Not only did her friends choose a throwaway as the overwhelming winner, but Kendra's top choice was not even among their favorites.

5. Create natural uses for words.

Inventing a word can give your brand a unique identity, but if the name is too unnatural, it could flop. Using a word from another language only works if the name is pronounceable. And if there are multiple ways to spell it, people will have a difficult time finding it online.

6. Use words that have a history with you.

Just as your dream has a history in your life, certain words carry greater meaning as well. Go with something you care about. Steve Jobs spent weekends during his college years working at an apple orchard, which resulted in the name of his company. And many start-ups in Silicon Valley are named after their founders' dogs.

7. Match the name to the personality.

Your name should reflect the personality of your organization. Using a play on words, such as "Skinny Dip Frozen Yogurt," suggests whimsy, whereas including the words "National" or "International" makes your brand feel weighty. There's a big difference in how people perceive "International Justice Mission" and "Not For Sale," even though both organizations have a similar purpose.

8. Adapt the name if necessary.

Sometimes the best names emerge from nicknames. Mark Zuckerberg changed the name of "The Facebook" to just "Facebook" at the suggestion of investor Sean Parker. The punk rock band MxPx began as Magnified Plaid. On one occasion, they wrote M.P. but used tiny x's instead of periods. Fans started calling them MxPx by mistake, but it was too late to correct everyone, so they kept the name.

One of Twitter's founders, Jack Dorsey, originally called his credit card payment system "Squirrel." It even came with a card reader in the shape of an acorn. But on a visit to the café at Apple's headquarters, he spotted a payment processing system with the same name. He promptly changed the name of his company to "Square."

THE STORIES BEHIND THE NAMES

Skype—the shortened version of "Sky Peer to Peer"

Wii—another way of saying "we" and depicts two "i's" playing together

TiVo—the combination of TV and "i" for input and "o" for output

eBay—a shortened version of the founding company, Echo Bay

Hulu—a Mandarin Chinese word for "interactive recording"

Hotmail—a snappy combination of "mail" and "HTML"

Twitter—a word that describes the sound of buzzing in people's pockets

Zynga—the name of the company founder's pet bulldog

Google—*googol* is the word for the number one followed by one hundred zeros

Yahoo!—came from the characters in Jonathan Swift's *Gulliver's Travels*

Apple—Steve Jobs worked at an apple orchard while he was in college

Pandora—came from the Greek goddess who received music gifts from Apollo

GoDaddy—an attempt to become memorable; "BigDaddy" was taken

Etsy—came from watching foreign films. It means "oh yes" in Italian

Step Away from the Photoshop

Your idea—no matter how brilliant—comes off as amateurish when you design it yourself. I don't care what the Mac revolution has done to put publishing tools in the hands of consumers; you're no artist. That is, unless you really are an artist. But even then, you could benefit from using someone better than you.

When I turned in the manuscript for my book to the publisher, the document looked disturbingly amateurish to me. The formatting in Microsoft Word felt like a research paper for school. The content didn't feel weighty like a book. But when the publisher returned page proofs that were designed by a professional typesetter, it looked exactly as a book should. It felt legitimate. My words seemingly grew in importance.

I do not dream at night, I dream all day, I dream for a living.

—STEVEN SPIELBERG

The same is true for your idea. Great design makes your work appear legitimate. Quality is the absence of nonquality cues. And whenever you play the designer, the probability of revealing nonquality cues goes through the roof.

I once attended an outdoor wedding where the father of the bride thought it would be a good idea to erect portable toilets around the lawn for the guests' convenience. Sure, it was easy, affordable, and convenient, but the wedding looked like a construction site and stank like an outhouse. He didn't pass his idea through the filter of design.

All of us have a bit of that father of the bride inside us. There are moments when we're tempted to do it ourselves because it's easier, cheaper, and more convenient. But if you have pride in your idea, take pride in how it's presented.

A great dream deserves great design.

HOW TO COMMISSION A LOGO

1. Communicate your preferences to the designer first

2. Receive a variety of options in black and white

3. Make sure there's a horizontal version and a "stacked" version

4. Tape the options to a wall to see which one looks best from a distance

5. Get feedback from your colleagues and friends

6. Make any adjustments to your favorite one

7. Request the colorized versions

8. Approve the final logo

9. Get multiple file types for use in various media

Create a Style Guide

The first time I hired a professional design firm to create a logo, they sent me the final product with a style guide. This was a rulebook for which colors, typefaces, and sizes I needed to use to portray my brand. They wanted to ensure that all of their hard work didn't go down the tubes because I decided to improvise.

Once you create a brand for your dream, improvisation is the enemy. A few tweaks here, a few additions there, and suddenly your brand looks as scattered as a NASCAR paint job. You need rules to keep your brand's integrity intact.

I can't tell you how many times I've seen a beautiful new Web site get butchered by a client who wanted to replace all of the images with his own.

Years ago, Coca-Cola had difficulty keeping its global team of designers on the same page. With ads running in more than two hundred countries, Coke's brand was plagued by inconsistencies. So the vice president of global design, David Butler, developed a book of standards that specified everything from the placement of the white ribbon that swirls down the side of the can to the kinds of clothes that models could wear in photo shoots. In other words, he created a rulebook.

To create a style guide, identify all of the qualities that characterize your brand and enforce them for a consistent experience. This applies to what colors you use, how your logo should appear, the "voice" in which you blog, how you answer the phone, and the manner in which you handle complaints. As the industrial designer Scott Wilson said, "Good design includes how you treat your customer."

Once you determine the essential ingredients for your brand, put them into action and guard them relentlessly. We become passionate about your dream only when you are. And you show your passion by how well you protect your brand. When you cut corners, we lose respect for it. But when you uphold your values, it grabs our attention and we begin to care too.

This is why my team always capitalizes the word STORY, even in text messages. And it's why we try to prevent anyone from slipping into our events for free. By upholding the value of the experience, we help other people uphold it too.

Take a few minutes to create your own style guide. Think back to the earliest ideas you had about your brand, the first feelings and impressions that swelled inside of you. Then write down how you want people to experience your dream as well. Start with four or five essential items. And be careful not to copy someone else's brand. Your experience should be yours and yours alone.

Your Communications Arsenal

Identify all the ways in which you'll communicate with your clients, community, or customers. Then ask a designer to create tools for those media. This way, you won't need a designer on an ongoing basis. It's a one-time purchase. These tools should be all you need to

communicate with your audience for the duration of the project. I
call it a "communications arsenal," and the tools can include:

1. Logo and key art
2. Promotional e-mail skins
3. Web site
4. Direct mail pieces
5. Brochures
6. ID badges
7. Signage
8. Stationery and business cards
9. Product packaging
10. Social media branding
11. Ads and posters

You'll save money by commissioning the entire arsenal, rather than
piecemealing it as you go along. And the designer can leverage the
same look and feel for each additional component, creating a consistency that will strengthen your brand.

How to Find a Designer

As the leader of your endeavor, you cannot afford to be uninformed
in this area. No matter what other responsibilities you have on your
plate, it pays to be a recruiter of artistic talent as well. A designer is
an integral part of your dream and how it's presented to the world.
This is not a role that should go to the first person who comes along.
It's important to find the right one.

Here are a few tips for finding a designer:

1. You'll find designers when you start looking for them.

Unless you're already in the practice of working with designers, they
can be hard to come by. But once you start looking, you'll find them
working from coffee shops, freelancing in their spare time, sharing

their work on Twitter, and running design studios. Ask your friends for connections. Survey other people in business. When you come across a Web site you like, check the site's credits for who designed it. Collect their business cards and examine their work. By comparing the options, you'll learn to distinguish design styles and find the right designer for your brand.

2. The portfolio shows you what they're capable of doing.

A designer's portfolio—or gallery of work—shows you not only the quality of their work, but also their style. Not every designer is suited for every kind of project. You can find a great designer who is absolutely wrong for your project. A designer is practically incapable of delivering a style that she's never created before. She will only give you what she is accustomed to creating. The clues are all there in the portfolio.

3. Not every designer is good at every kind of medium.

Some designers are great at page layout and typesetting but struggle with Web sites. Other designers are great at compositing photos but can't design a clean brochure. And you can tell pretty quickly whether someone is good at creating logos. A mediocre logo designer will use stock typefaces and borrowed icons to piece together an identity, whereas a great logo designer will create a unique and customized mark.

4. Prices vary from designer to designer.

I have never paid the same amount for any designer. My designer friend in southern California charges $200 an hour. Another friend in Anderson, South Carolina, charges $100 an hour. A designer in northern Virginia charges $40 an hour. A studio in Atlanta doesn't charge by the hour, but by the project. An Oklahoma friend once designed my Web site for free. Another designer gives me a cost estimate but tells me to make a counteroffer if it doesn't fit my budget.

As you start working with more designers, you'll get a feel for the going rates.

5. Identify great designs and then find the designer.

Designers often place a link to their own Web sites on the sites they create as a way to attract more clients. You can also search online portfolios such as Dribbble.com and Behance.net to find quality designers. But keep in mind you're not just hiring their work; you're also hiring their work style. It's important to find someone you enjoy working with and who understands your vision for the project.

6. Have a clear vision for your project.

When you talk to a designer about your project, be clear about what you want. It's not their job to define your project. That's your job. If you give them a list of needs without any further explanation, you won't get your vision for the project; you'll get theirs. Sometimes designers provide a questionnaire that draws out your vision, but the onus is on you. Let them know the look and feel you're going for. Otherwise, it'll be frustrating for everyone when you hate the first, second, and third round of designs.

Negotiating Design

Many Dream Year participants are designers; so let me speak out of both sides of my mouth for a moment. One of the first rules of monetizing your dream is to charge profitable rates. So if you're a designer, your goal is to raise your fee as high as you can. But for the rest of us, design is an operational expense, which must be reduced.

To negotiate well, you have to know the cost of design, which is something only experience can bring. Get a feel for the market. Ask questions. Inquire about fees. Find out the going rates. The reason many firms can charge so much for design is because clients are clueless about the alternatives. If you hire a large design firm, know that you're paying premium prices to cover the company's business expenses. And while you'll save money with a freelancer, know that customer service might suffer while the designer is working a full-time job or juggling multiple projects.

Most designers charge an hourly fee, but you can also propose a flat rate for projects so there are no surprises at the end. When you create a budget, decide how much you can spend on design, and then spend only that. I've been turned down by offering too little for a project. But sometimes it pays off. I've had designers fall in love with a project and spend more time on it than I could have possibly paid them by the hour.

Sometimes you can offer value besides money.

I once asked a designer to create a project at half his usual rate. I sealed the deal by offering him exposure at my next event. It was a win for both of us. He grew my brand, and I grew his platform. Think about what you might be able to offer in exchange for design work. Accounting services? Chiropractic care? Free smoothies?

Whenever I find good designers, I try to increase what I pay them as we continue to work together so they know I'm working to fulfill not just my dream, but theirs as well. Good designers are hard to find, so it pays to keep them happy.

What happens if you pay for a project but hate the work?

First, make sure the design is presented to you in stages. Don't let the designer work in secret for months without showing you anything. Set milestones so you can see the work in progress. This way, it can't go too far in the wrong direction. That goes for the fees as well. Pay in stages rather than one lump sum up front. Otherwise, you'll have less room to negotiate if you hate the work the designer presents.

Second, don't settle for bad design. If you don't like the work, be considerate, but let the designer know it's not working for you. Designers want to please you as much as you want to be pleased. They'll likely keep working until they get it right.

Third, if the corrections still don't satisfy you, offer to pay a "kill fee" and end the project. This is a fee for the work the designer has done, but not the full amount. You can either establish this fee in the initial agreement or negotiate it later. But you'll ruin your reputation by walking away from incomplete projects without paying anything. It's no fun to pay for a project you can't use, but you'll save face, keep a good reputation, and make a clean break so you can find someone new.

Call to Action

Branding is not just about the logo and design. It's about the total user experience for your dream. There is no greater privilege than creating a whole new experience for people to enjoy. Whether you're creating a new retail space, a new product, a charity, or a service-oriented business, you get to determine how people will interact with your dream every step of the way. First, you have to imagine it.

Here is your assignment—create a branding manifesto for your dream. What will it smell like? What colors will dominate your environment? How will you answer the phone? What music will play in the background? How will it feel to the touch? What will you not include? Remember, it's not just about what you include. It's also about what you exclude. Create a brand experience for your dream.

After you define the brand experience, create a style guide. This is essentially a rulebook for you and other team members to follow. Once you create the brand, protect it from improvisation. Not everything is up for debate or interpretation. Protect your brand with an iron fist.

Finally, after you've defined your style guide, list those items in your communications arsenal. This is a collection of media in which you'll communicate with your audience. It could include signage, letterhead, e-mail templates, your Web site, and printed brochures, among other things. Not only will you save money by contracting a designer to produce all of it at once, but you'll also maintain visual consistency in all of your correspondence. You'll come off more intentional, more professional.

QUESTIONS:

1. Where can you start looking for designers? Begin collecting contacts and start reviewing their portfolios. Can you see the differences in style?

2. It's important to know what you want before approaching a designer. What would you say to a designer if she asked you what you were looking for?

3. What are the rules that will govern your brand? What qualities will define your total "user experience"?

BUILDING YOUR PLATFORM

Extraordinary things are done by communities of passion.
....
—GARY HAMEL

No One Cares About Your Cause

It doesn't matter how noble your dream is. If you don't have a platform, no one cares about your idea.

You can set out to stop sex trafficking, grant microloans to struggling entrepreneurs in Africa, work to prevent the spread of AIDS, or raise money to help the homeless—all worthy endeavors for sure. But without a platform, your cause will go nowhere. And unfortunately, when most people try to launch a new initiative, building a platform is the area in which they struggle the most.

They have great ideas but no audience.

There are too many businesses, nonprofits, ideas, and charities vying for attention. People don't have time to research all of the options. So they look for the most popular brands and contribute to those endeavors.

The winners keep winning and the losers keep losing. It's the way of the social economy. People only care about things that matter to other people.

Too many of us take a "field of dreams" approach to our ideas.

We think that if we just build it, they will come. But it's not the idea that spreads as much as it is the social movement behind it.

Don't worry about people stealing your ideas. If your ideas are any good, you'll have to ram them down people's throats.

—HOWARD AIKEN

In 2006, musician and filmmaker Steve Taylor from Nashville set out to turn author Donald Miller's best-selling book *Blue Like Jazz* into a movie. He spent four years trying to raise money until two investors finally agreed to provide $250,000 each. However, the day before preproduction started, one of the investors backed out and the project was scrapped.

When two fans of the book, Jonathan Frazier and Zach Prichard from Nashville, heard the bad news, they decided to launch a Kickstarter campaign to raise $125,000 to save the project. But after three days, they had raised only $300. It appeared that no one cared about their cause. After all, they had no platform.

But then everything changed.

Five days after the Kickstarter project launched, Donald Miller got involved and wrote about the campaign on his own blog. A month later, on October 25, 2010, the project had taken in $345,992, which was the largest amount ever raised on Kickstarter until that date. It was the same project, the same idea, and the same cause, but Donald Miller's platform put it over the top.

A platform is the community of people who follow you. They pay attention to what you say or do. They care about your opinions. They subscribe to your offerings. They buy your products and they share your interests. It can include your social media following, your network of friends, your existing customers, or the fans of your work. But without these supporters, your idea will go nowhere.

Matthew Cardona is a professional wrestler in the WWE who goes by the name of Zack Ryder. In 2011, Matt realized he wasn't going anywhere in the league. They weren't putting him on television, and without airtime, he knew his time was running out. He had nothing to lose. So Matt attempted something that would either reinvigorate his career or get him fired. He started promoting himself as "the Internet champion of the world." He posted videos of himself on YouTube, made himself a fake title belt, and asked his fans on social media to lobby the WWE for more airtime.

The gamble paid off.

Matt's videos grew to 11 million views, and fans everywhere started wearing Zack Ryder T-shirts and waving signs at his matches. As people rallied around Matt, the WWE took notice and gave him more time on air. His career exploded, and he became a regular feature on WWE's *Raw* TV show.

"I realized I wasn't going anywhere in the WWE, and if I was going out, I was going to go out swinging," Matt said. "I thought—this will either get me noticed and back on TV or get me fired. It was a risk I was willing to take. A year later, it saved my career. Unbelievable."

If you lack a platform right now, you have five options:

1. Start building one now.

The best time to build a platform was last year. The next best time is now. Start a blog, a monthly e-mail newsletter, a Twitter account, a Facebook page, a YouTube channel, a digital magazine, or even a series of meet-ups. Find the best medium for your gifts, and create a way for people to join your tribe. If you provide quality content and meaningful interaction on a regular basis, you'll build a following over time. You'll have to devote time to it each day, but the social investment will make it easier to launch your offering when the time is right.

2. Tap into your friends.

Even if you don't have a huge following, your friends have platforms that amount to something more substantial. When I launched my first conference, I only had a blog to promote it. So I asked a hundred online friends to help me spread the word. Within just a few hours, I counted hundreds of mentions on social media that represented tens of thousands of readers. But remember—you have to ask. I advise everyone in the Dream Year coaching program to spend an entire day making all of the necessary asks to launch well. You can track your social reach with tools such as SumAll.com, SproutSocial .com, and Sendible.com.

3. Borrow it from others.

If you're an aspiring author who doesn't have a large enough platform to get published, consider a collaborative approach that invites other influencers to contribute to the book. In 2010, social media consultant Tim Schraeder from Chicago launched a book on communications called *Outspoken* that features chapters from more than sixty experts. Because the contributors promoted the book on their own platforms, it sold 1,200 copies in five days. Sometimes you have to borrow other people's platforms until you build your own.

4. Pay for it.

If you don't have your own platform, you can certainly buy one. You can pay for advertising, social media mentions, Facebook boosts, or product placement. But buying a platform lacks an emotional connection to your audience, converting these relationships into sales isn't guaranteed, and the rates can be costly. But if you have the budget and no other way to get your message out, it's a great way to get eyeballs on your brand.

5. Pitch it to the media.

Find a newsworthy angle and pitch your story to journalists. They're not interested in promoting your organization (they'll send you to the advertising department for that). They're looking for larger societal issues, such as interesting new research, solutions to a community problem, or industry trends.

For example, if you're launching a catering business, you could submit a press release about how curated dinner parties among friends are sweeping the country. You would include your business as part of the story, along with other examples.

In 2010, Dream Year Weekend participant Mica May lobbied a producer at ABC's *Good Morning America* for months to feature her custom monogrammed journals called "May Books." It wasn't until the show was putting together its annual gift-buying episode for Christmas that the journals became newsworthy. The show featured the journals, and Mica sold more than thirty thousand products within the month.

Become the World's Leading Expert

You build a platform by delivering value on a consistent basis in the area of your expertise. The more specific it is, the better. In fact, you should be able to describe it with just one word.

For Seth Godin, it's marketing. For Anthony Robbins, it's motivation. Oprah dominates interviews. John Grisham owns the legal category. And Stephen King rules horror. We view these people as the world's leading experts in their fields.

When you own a category, other people are forced to take a different approach to the same craft. After David Copperfield established himself as the leading stage magician in the 1990s, David Blaine had to master street illusions. Criss Angel had to take a mystical approach. Nobody else could do what David Copperfield did because he already dominated it.

At the 2011 Dartmouth College commencement, comedian Conan O'Brien talked about the need for new categories in the same industry:

Way back in the 1940s, there was a very funny man by the name of Jack Benny. He was a giant star—easily one of the greatest comedians of his generation. And a much younger man named Johnny Carson wanted very much to be Jack Benny. In some ways, he was, but in many ways, he wasn't. He emulated Jack Benny, but his own quirks and mannerisms, along with the changing medium, pulled him in a different direction. And yet, his failure to completely become his hero made him the funniest person of his generation. David Letterman wanted to be Johnny Carson, and was not. And as a result, my generation of comedians wanted to be David Letterman. And none of us are. My peers and I have all missed that mark in a thousand different ways. But the point is this—it is our failure to become our perceived ideal that ultimately defines us and makes us unique.

Our tendency is to enter a field and emulate the experts in an effort to be taken seriously. But this only leaves us overlooked and ignored.

The former editor in chief of *Salon* Kerry Lauerman described how the publication found itself in an economic downturn several years ago. They resorted to the same cost-cutting tactics as other online magazines—fewer writers, faster delivery, and more content aggregation, which is the act of linking to articles on other sites. The approach saved money, but *Salon*'s readership and revenue tanked. *Salon* was being ignored in the sea of everybody else.

It wasn't until *Salon* had the courage to embrace its expertise— writing longer, more thoughtful, original pieces—that it found its core audience again. The publication ended 2011 with 7 million unique visitors for the first time in the company's history, and page views are still climbing.

What is your field of expertise? If you're an author, what kind of books will you write? If you're a humanitarian, what is the one specialty that will define you? And if you're in the business community, what is your one specialized deliverable? You'll need one if you hope to be noticed.

Think about your word. What is the one word that people might use to describe you? Take a minute to fill in this blank:

I am the _____ guy.

Or

I am the _____ gal.

You are the world's leading expert at something. You may not know what it is yet, but once you find it, your skill and focus in that one area will build a tremendous platform for you. Until then, your lack of clarity is sabotaging you.

Your first 10,000 photographs are your worst.

—HENRI CARTIER-BRESSON

In 1998, Sara Blakely from Atlanta made history when she chopped the feet off her pantyhose so she could enhance her figure without the stockings visible. She had inadvertently created a new industry for footless hosiery. In 2000, she launched Spanx and by 2010 had sold more than 6 million pairs of her new creation. But Sara's success came from embracing one expertise. She said, "I keep saying this to the team: 'We've got to own something.'" Sara's expertise just happened to be butts.

When you know your greatest strength, it's much easier to build a tribe. Narrowing your focus doesn't limit your opportunities; it expands them. People flock to specialists.

I believe that every person can be the best in the world at one thing. The trouble is we enter categories that are too broad. We write books on subjects that have been addressed in thousands of others. We launch nonprofits that tackle the same issues as everyone else. And we start companies that look no different from all the rest.

Do you know that one area in which you are the world's leading expert? It's a small niche. It's a tiny slice. It's so offbeat that no one else could have imagined it. In fact, it probably hasn't been invented yet.

It's creating clever doodles on index cards like Jessica Hagy.

It's writing love letters to strangers in NYC like Hannah Brencher.

It's acting like a pretentious theater arts student like Colleen Ballinger.

It's cloning yourself in homemade dance videos like Elle Walker.

Each of these people undertook a unique activity that no one else was doing and became the world's leading expert at it. Their singular focus has led to thousands of followers on social media, corporate sponsorships, book deals, and media exposure.

It's impossible to be the best in the world at being a generalist.

How to Land Speaking Engagements

Speaking at events is another way to build your platform, as well as generate additional income. But it's not easy to get these opportunities. You're competing with a lot of talented people, along with a lot of ambitious people who are not so talented. Here are some ways to set yourself apart and land engagements:

1. Become known for stark, compelling ideas.

Nancy Duarte has mastered the topic of presentations. Seth Godin brings clarity to getting noticed in a crowded marketplace. Timothy Ferriss is famous for advocating the four-hour workweek. And Malcolm Gladwell offers a fascinating perspective on social movements. These communicators are known for compelling ideas that allow them to command substantial speaking fees. What is the stark, compelling idea for which you will be known? It goes back to knowing your one expertise.

2. Work on improving your speaking ability.

Organizers book speakers for compelling ideas. Speaking ability is often a secondary consideration. But if you want to build a career out of speaking, it helps to get better at it. Practice your craft. Take a speaking course. Read books on presenting. Watch famous speeches. Rehearse your talk on camera. And get feedback from others. Speaking opportunities beget speaking opportunities when you deliver excellence.

3. Have someone else recommend you.

I know it's tempting, but fight the urge to appeal directly to conference organizers. Presumptuous people approach them all the time to be considered for a slot, and you don't want to be one of them. It comes off as desperate at best and arrogant at worst. It's better to have someone of influence recommend you, whether it's a trusted friend or a speaking agent. You'll be taken more seriously.

4. Do interesting things.

Speaking opportunities don't come from being available. They come from doing noteworthy things. If you want to inspire teenagers from the stage, start by investing in the ones in your community. If you have an interesting life story, start sharing it in articles, blog posts, and videos. Or create your own events. No one wants to book a desperate speaker who is begging for opportunities. Organizers want to catch someone in the act of greatness.

5. Determine what will define your speaking career.

Don't overlook your personal brand when a speaking opportunity comes along. Decide whether you'll speak at breakouts or just keynotes, how much you require for a speaking fee, the environment for your presentation, and even the minimum crowd size. If you let other people determine these factors, your reputation will rest in their hands. Make a list of the factors you need because, like your brand, everything communicates something.

6. Have someone else handle the negotiation.

You don't need a professional booking agent. But if you have someone else handle the negotiations, it will save you from being the bad guy. Give your representative a list of your conditions and availability and let them work out the details. You can offer a commission or ask a friend to help you for free. But you'll appear more professional and be able to respond more objectively to each request.

1,000 True Fans

Wired cofounder Kevin Kelly advocates a principle called "1,000 True Fans." He says that anyone who produces works of art needs to accumulate only one thousand true fans in order to earn a living. This goes for artists as well as entrepreneurs, advocates, and authors. All you need is an offering for $50, $100, or more each year, and you can sustain a livelihood with one thousand customers.

The goal of one thousand people sounds reasonable, but how do you reach it?

Think about the kind of "following" you want to build. What kind of people are they? How do they think and where do you find them? It's as much about what you *don't* do as it is about what you do.

Here are some questions to ask yourself. There are no right or wrong answers. Your response doesn't matter as much as the thinking it exposes. There is a particular mind-set that's required to build a platform. This process will define how you interact with people and what kind of fans you'll attract.

If you owned a carpet store, which approach would you rather take?

a. Advertise a clearance sale every weekend for high-volume sales.
b. Sell only the finest carpets to the most discriminating clients.

If you owned a restaurant, which approach would you rather take?

a. A fast-food chain that sells discounted food in large quantities.
b. A themed restaurant that sells ambiance as much as it sells food.

If you were a real estate agent, what kind of listings would you prefer?

a. Apartments in high-density neighborhoods off the interstate.
b. Exclusive homes in an area where you might sell only a few each year.

If you were a movie director, what kind of films would you rather produce?

a. Slapstick comedies with sophomoric college humor.
b. Epic movies based on serious historical themes.

When building a platform, the temptation is to go with every conceivable tactic to gain a following. But what attracts some people will repel others. You define whom you reach by what you *don't* do.

In May 2006, a farmer's wife named Ree Drummond found herself alone in the Oklahoma farmhouse where she homeschooled her children. Her husband had taken their four kids out to the fields for a few hours to give her a break.

Ree had grown used to the solitary life of a rancher, but it hadn't always been that way. Growing up, she was the daughter of an orthopedic surgeon and vacationed each summer in Hilton Head, South Carolina. She attended the University of Southern California to study broadcast journalism in hopes of becoming the next Jane Pauley. But on a trip home to see her family during a school break, she met a mysterious and rugged man at a bar who swept her off her feet and into the life of a farming, homeschooling housewife and mother.

On that morning, when "The Marlboro Man," as she affectionately calls him, took the kids out to the fields, Ree decided to start a blog where she could keep in touch with her family in other parts of the country. She called herself "The Pioneer Woman" and described her adventures of living on a farm. She took photos of her surroundings and wrote about her life—her children, her cattle, her cooking, and her husband, whom she never mentions by name. Her reader-ship soared.

Within a year, she received the "Best Kept Secret Award" at the 2007 Bloggies. In 2009, she won the Best Photography and Best-Designed Weblog categories, along with Weblog of the Year. By 2011, she was getting 23.3 million page views each month and 4.4 million unique visitors. Her advertising revenue alone brought in more than $1 million a year.

But Ree's approach is what sets her apart. She doesn't write about politics or take sarcastic jabs at other people. She doesn't try to shock people into reading her blog. Her tone is always jovial and upbeat, if not cheesy at times. She tells stories about her kids and the personalities of her cows. She posts step-by-step instructions on how to sear steaks the proper way and how to make smoothies—all demonstrated with beautiful photos. She appeals to her audience by portraying a life of simplicity, good food, and love of family.

Ree has gone on to release a romance novel, four children's books, and three cookbooks in a series called *The Pioneer Woman Cooks*, which have become *New York Times* bestsellers. She even got her own television show on the Food Network.

All of this has come from knowing exactly who is in her target audience and who is not. Ree admitted that her readership is 95 percent female. These readers have become the true fans that sustain her livelihood.

As you build your platform, you don't have to send mass e-mails to strangers or follow everyone on Twitter hoping they'll follow you back. You don't have to create a blog for everyone. You can be more discriminating. You can cut out certain types of people and limit your audience. It's counterintuitive, but you'll create a more loyal fan base by *not* aiming for everyone. Don't seek the masses. Find your one thousand true fans first, and the masses will come.

Choose Your Medium

Building a platform is not about becoming famous. It's about building a distribution channel for your dream. Just as railroad companies in the 1800s laid tracks out west to carry supplies for new homes and businesses, your platform is a distribution channel that brings your gift to the world. If you don't have a platform, you'll always be at the mercy of promoting your offerings through those who do.

In the 1990s, billionaire Phil Anschutz began acquiring railroads throughout the country. You wouldn't think of railroads as the best investment in the modern age, but Phil had a vision for something bigger. He used the hundreds of thousands of miles of track, which connected every major city, to lay fiber-optic cable. He didn't buy the railways for the train systems. He bought them to create a distribution channel for digital entertainment.

Phil acquired Regal CineMedia, which included more than 400 movie theaters, representing roughly 4,900 screens. Phil intended to build a "digital content network" that was capable of receiving, storing, and digitally projecting alternative content to his chain of movie theaters, such as live concerts and sporting events. Conveniently, Phil also owns the O2 Arena in London, the Staples Center, several professional soccer teams, and a stake in the Los Angeles Lakers and the L.A. Kings hockey team.

I'm for the dreamers. The only really important things in history have been started by dreamers. They never know what can't be done.

—BILL VEECK

When you build your own platform, you can go straight to people with your offerings. You don't have to be a glorified beggar, asking every blogger, influencer, or media outlet to talk about your idea. You own the network.

Building a platform is not the same as starting a blog. It can be.

But never confuse a platform with social media. You don't have to start a blog, a Twitter account, or a Facebook page if that's not your thing. You can just as easily cultivate a following offline. The truth is, not everyone can be a great blogger. Some people write better with 70,000 words than 140 characters.

Novelist Stephen King once tweeted: "On Twitter at last, and can't think of a thing to say. Some writer I turned out to be."

Some people can't write well at all, but they're great on video. Some people build platforms with the products they create or the performances they give. Others aren't on social media but have thousands of fans because of their ability to connect. So don't beat yourself up if your blog readership consists of no more than your adoring mother and lurking boss. You can be great at something else.

Here are some other platforms that have worked for other people:

Video

On July 9, 2010, a twenty-three-year-old bartender named Jenna Mourey from Cambridge, Massachusetts, was getting ready for work when she turned on a camera and recorded a humorous self-help video called "How to Trick People into Thinking You're Good Looking." In a deadpan voice, she demonstrated how she turned herself from ordinary to eye-catching using cosmetic tricks, such as spray tanning, bleached hair, caked-on makeup, black eye shadow, and painted-on eyebrows.

After transforming herself on camera, Jenna demonstrated how *not* to act in public, explaining that "since you were born ugly, you're probably pretty weird." The video ended with Jenna pretending to cry over her unused master's diploma.

The video took off among her own social network over the weekend but then went viral, generating more than 55 million views, and turned Jenna into a YouTube sensation. Jenna continues to make videos under the name Jenna Marbles (her dog's name) with subjects such as "How to Avoid Talking to People You Don't Want to Talk To" and "What Girls Do in the Car."

Her audience is mostly thirteen-year-old girls, but she's got nearly 12 million subscribers on YouTube, and the video ad buying company TubeMogul estimates that in 2012 she could have earned nearly $350,000 from advertising revenue alone.

You never know what kind of platform you can build until you turn on the camera. You only need to hit "record" and post the results to Vine, Instagram, Vimeo, or YouTube.

Products

Quality products can amass a following as well. Workmanship builds platform. Ben Cohen and Jerry Greenfield created a fan base around Ben & Jerry's ice cream. Zappos developed a cultlike following by "delivering happiness" with exceptional customer service. I have an instant connection with people who use Moleskine journals like me. And while Steve Jobs never owned a blog or a Twitter account, there are millions of people who have practically turned him into a patron saint.

Smart companies don't just sell products; they build communities. How can you give your customers a sense of belonging with your brand? How can you move people from a transactional relationship where they're simply buying your thing to a personal relationship where they're identifying with you? You want them to feel like co-owners and ambassadors of the brand. You could provide upgrades to your best customers when they least expect it, surprise clients with special gifts in the mail, or offer a membership program to your most loyal followers.

Amazon has built a platform around Amazon Prime. This annual membership gives customers free shipping, faster delivery, and access to more than eleven thousand streaming movies and TV shows for an annual fee of $99. The company won't say how many members there are, but analysts put it at 10 million people and speculate that it could grow to 25 million by 2017. Amazon Prime has become an identity for its best customers, a way for them to become part of the inner circle.

Performances

If you're good at what you do, share it with the world. You can't build a tribe until you give people something to rally around. There's a perfect medium for your craft, whether it's a podcast, a Pinterest account, an Instagram feed, or a YouTube channel.

Pop superstar Justin Bieber got started by posting homemade music videos on YouTube. Teenage musician Christofer Drew Ingle from Joplin, Missouri, who performs as the leader of the band Never Shout Never, was discovered on Myspace. Andy Samberg landed a job on *Saturday Night Live* by posting humorous videos of his comedy troupe The Lonely Island on YouTube.

Even dancers are doing it. Marquese Scott masters a unique style of dancing to dubstep music, with its overwhelming bass lines and reverberant drum patterns. He can move like a robot, appearing to dance in slow motion and even backward, as if someone were reversing his movements on video.

Marquese had been posting videos of himself dancing on YouTube since 2003 with little fanfare. But on September 23, 2011, he posted his fifty-third video that showed him dancing to a remixed version of the song "Pumped Up Kicks" by the band Foster the People. The next morning, it had gotten more than 10 million hits. By the fourth month, there were 30 million views. And by the printing of this book, there have been more than 103 million views. It opened the door for him to appear on numerous television shows and get booked as a dancer all over the world.

Network of Friends

After graduating from New York University, Scott Harrison spent ten years promoting nightclubs and fashion events. He partied with models and New York socialites, taking heavy drugs and living what he calls a selfish and decadent life.

But on a trip to Uruguay at the age of twenty-eight, Scott came to the end of himself and resolved to do something better with his life. He quit his job and volunteered for thirteen months as a photojournalist for Mercy Ships, which sends doctors to provide free health care to developing countries.

Scott learned that 80 percent of the diseases he encountered were caused by unsafe water and poor sanitation, so he decided to do something about it.

On his thirty-first birthday, September 7, 2006, he invited his friends to a party in New York where he encouraged them to donate $20 for clean drinking water rather than buy him gifts. By the end of the night, they had raised $15,000, which went toward fixing three wells and building three new ones at a refugee camp in Uganda.

His organization, charity: water, was born.

Scott had unknowingly built a platform for his charity by working as a nightclub promoter all those years. He didn't abandon the social network after his lifestyle and values changed. He leveraged the influence that was already at his disposal.

Self-Published Books

At the age of seventeen, Amanda Hocking from Austin, Minnesota, began sending query letters to publishers for her novels. But, for the next eight years, she was rejected by each and every one of them. In March 2010, as a last-ditch effort to raise $350 for a trip to Chicago, Amanda published her own e-book on Amazon called *My Blood Approves* about a vampire love triangle. Six months later, more than 150,000 copies had sold for a total of $20,000. By 2011, she had uploaded all of her novels and was selling 9,000 books a day. She made the *USA Today* bestseller list without a publisher and stayed there for fifty weeks. After she sold 1.5 million copies of her books, grossing $2 million in sales, publishers finally took notice, and she was offered a multimillion-dollar contract with St. Martin's Press.

Self-publishing your own book is no guarantee of success, but it allows you to rally fans around your work. Amanda confessed that she had a difficult childhood with the divorce of her parents and her mother's ensuing poverty. She spent a lot of time crying in her room with reading as her only escape. When she started writing, it was

about a world unlike her own. She wrote about mythological creatures and magical powers with characters that faced real issues like
pain, sorrow, and love. By creating her own fantasy stories, Amanda
had unknowingly tapped into a market with millions of passionate
readers.

Events

In 2008, Elliott Bisnow was publishing real estate magazines with his
father in Washington, D.C., when he decided to start networking
with other entrepreneurs. He invited the founders of CollegeHumor
.com, Josh Abramson and Ricky Van Veen, to join him for an all-
expenses paid trip to Park City, Utah, to ski and connect with other
entrepreneurs. Elliott put the trip on credit cards hoping that the
relationships would turn into bigger opportunities. After another
successful event in Mexico, Elliott realized he was onto something
and started a biannual gathering of entrepreneurs called Summit
Series. In 2011, the event was ranked by *Fast Company* as one of the
top business gatherings in the country.

Hosting events rallies people not only around your cause, but
also to one another, which is an infinitely more powerful outcome.
It can feel like you're serving only other people's interests, connect-
ing them to one another and highlighting other experts at the expense of your own platform, but you'll get the credit. You'll become
the tribal leader. As your event grows, you can offer your own resources, sell your own products, and launch your own initiatives to
a ready-made audience.

Build a Mailing List

Being on social media is one thing. It allows people to visit your site
and rally around your offering. But occasionally, you'll need a mailing list to go to them. This is a direct line of communication that
your audience has permitted you to use—not to abuse—when necessary.

When you have a mailing list, advertising becomes obsolete. You don't need to pay for access to someone else's community because you already have your own.

Web guru Chris Brogan wrote, "You live or die by your database. . . . I work every day on building my email newsletter list because if I can offer you recurring value there, I'll have the opportunity to reach out to you when I've got something else that you'll find useful later on. If you're not working on lists as part of your social media efforts, you're missing an opportunity."

You build a mailing list by harvesting contact information. The first time I promoted an event, I started with a list of two hundred e-mail addresses that I had collected from business cards, longtime friends, colleagues, and coworkers. The success of that meager list turned me into the "chief e-mail gatherer" of my company.

There are two ways to harvest contact information.

One way is to collect information by any means possible. You borrow it, steal it, rent it, or trade it with other people. It's a horrible method because those people never gave you permission to contact them. They not only don't want anything from you—they don't want to hear from you. It's a cold approach.

The other way (and best way) to build a mailing list is to cultivate your own tribe of people who opt in. You do this by offering something of value in exchange for their willingness to hear from you again. Not only did they give you permission to contact them, they're looking forward to it. This is a warm approach.

For each of my events, I often promote a sweepstakes to collect contact information from prospective attendees. In the first year of STORY, I gave away an all-expenses-paid trip to Oxford, England, and a five-day stay in C. S. Lewis's famous home The Kilns to a lucky winner. I didn't do it to be nice. I was trying to collect data. The giveaway generated thousands of e-mail addresses from people who opted in. They gladly offered their information for a chance to win the trip and hear from us again.

I was inspired to offer giveaways because in 2006 my wife, Ainsley, and I won an all-expenses-paid trip to London through a national sweepstakes from Kodak. They asked for my information at a mall kiosk, and I gladly gave up my privacy for a chance of winning the trip. Thankfully, it paid off.

A software company called Logos in Bellingham, Washington, owns hundreds of Web sites whose sole intent is to harvest e-mail addresses for their marketing efforts. They offer online giveaways and scholarships in various categories to capture contact information from the entrants. The data goes right into their mailing lists where they can send promotions for their products and services.

Contests aren't the only way to build a mailing list. You can also offer content-rich media, such as e-newsletters, PDF books, training courses, music, and downloads.

In 2010, one of Dream Year's participants, Josh Brickey, started a ministry in Columbia, South Carolina, called The Venue. He had few contacts in the community, so on Independence Day, he and a dozen volunteers filmed hundreds of people telling their life stories at a community festival. They gave each participant a card that pointed them to a Web site called Stories of Columbia where they could watch everyone's videos. Joshua not only served the community; he also got their contact information.

Improve Your Ground Game

One of the ways that political experts said Barack Obama beat Mitt Romney in the 2012 presidential election was by creating a better distribution channel. The Romney campaign hired only five hundred national employees, whereas the Obama campaign hired more than three thousand workers nationwide and recruited hundreds of thousands of volunteers.

President Obama's goal was to get as close to voters as possible. He set up a "barbershop and beauty salon" strategy to get people to register to vote when they went for haircuts. "Faith captains" were assigned to churches, and "condo captains" were encouraged to know everyone in their buildings.

With so many workers on Obama's team, he didn't have to rely so much on advertising. Each worker was responsible for about fifty voters in key precincts, whereas Romney's workers had to reach thousands of voters in order to succeed.

Not only this, but Obama's team launched a Facebook app that was downloaded by more than 1 million supporters. Roughly one out of every five users who were asked to share about the campaign did so with their Facebook friends.

Obama built a platform.

Think of your dream like a presidential campaign. How can you get close to your customers, donors, readers, voters, or clients long before you need them?

Building a platform is about getting people to care. And you don't get them to care by blasting out your own ideas and opinions at the expense of theirs. You do it by offering value, meeting a need, or solving a problem. You might be most effective at posting updates on Facebook or by uploading photos on Instagram. Maybe you're better with passionate e-mails to a growing mailing list. But one thing is for sure: you've got to improve your ground game in order to succeed.

Call to Action

Most people launch their dreams without a platform and, as a result, end up reaching no one. People only take notice of you when you're the best in the world at something and then offer value to them on a repeated basis over time. So answer this question—in what area are you the world's leading expert?

You should be able to identify it with one word. You are either the _____ guy or the _____ gal. Wrestle with this question. Write it down. Don't go any further until you can identify your expertise.

Next, determine how you will start offering value to the world in your area of expertise. Will you shoot videos for YouTube? Will you start a blog? How about a monthly e-newsletter? Maybe your preference is live events or meet-ups. Some people just need a phone to make a lot of personal connections.

No matter what you do, offer value on a consistent basis, and the people who care will come rallying around you. Your platform will begin to take shape.

Finally, figure out a way to start capturing people's contact information, especially their e-mail addresses. Blogging and podcasting enable people to come to you for value, but sometimes you need to be able to go to them. A growing e-mail list will allow you to reach out on your terms. And if you've spent enough time building relational capital, they won't mind hearing from you at all.

QUESTIONS:

1. You are the best in the world at one thing. What is the one word that best defines you? Can you define it?
2. As you attempt to cultivate one thousand true fans, what kind of people do you want to attract? What kind of people do you *not* want to attract?
3. What opportunities are you missing by not building a mailing list? What is the best way for you to begin growing a mailing list?

MARKETING YOUR DREAM

Anything that won't sell, I don't want to invent. Its sale is proof of utility, and utility is success.

—THOMAS A. EDISON

Marketing Versus Sales

You came into this year as a visionary, but you're going to leave it as the chief marketing officer for your dream. What good is an idea if nobody knows about it?

The pie maker cannot avoid becoming the pie marketer. The author cannot avoid becoming the advertiser. And the service provider cannot avoid becoming the service promoter.

Launching your dream requires one of two activities: sales or marketing. Marketing is the act of creating demand for your offering. This happens through branding, product development, design, platform building, advertising, and word of mouth, among other things. Marketing is the work of creating interest within potential customers.

Marketing is fun.

It's the idea model you create, the blog posts you write, the designs you make, the ads you place, and the buzz you build. If you do it well, you won't need to sell anything. People will come to you.

Sales, on the other hand, is no fun at all.

Sales is the work of persuading someone to buy your product or service. You appeal to the benefits of your offering, counter objections, and answer people's questions in hopes of talking them into it.

You don't want to be in sales. Who wants to be in the business of trying to persuade someone to do something they don't want to do?

Sales means they don't want it yet.

Sales means there is currently no demand for it.

Sales means they don't believe they need it.

Sales means there is no social validation.

If you find yourself trying to "sell" your dream to other people, it means there's not enough demand for it yet. You can keep making pitches. You can keep knocking on doors and making phone calls. It's a numbers game. Eventually, someone will buy. But it's better to build demand for your dream and let sales come to you.

Creating Demand

Every so often, an idea comes along that people cannot resist. It meets their desires, satisfies a niche, and comes at the perfect moment in history all at once. As Victor Hugo said, "Nothing is as powerful as an idea whose time has come." Creating demand isn't easy. Success often surprises the creator as much as anyone else. But here are several things you can do to help your dream along if it's not taking off:

1. Revisit your idea model.

Adjust your idea model until it connects with people. Change the location, the date, the price, or the name. Change each element and measure the results until you get it right. No ideas are sacred, especially unsuccessful ones.

2. Revisit your branding.

Perceptions matter. People can tell if you designed your Web site yourself, which comes off as amateurish, or if you've hired a professional. If you're trying to convey excellence, people have to perceive it first through your branding. Put it in the hands of a designer.

3. Revisit your platform.

When you don't have an audience, great ideas go unnoticed. Spend a little time each day building your tribe. Offer something of value to your followers on a consistent basis and interact with them in a meaningful way. Be careful not to settle into a platform that's going nowhere. Take risks to grow your audience.

When Frans Johansson released his book *The Medici Effect* in 2006, the market was saturated with books about innovation. Frans was a first-time author and only two years out of business school. Knowing that a great idea isn't enough to make it successful, he took a different route to creating demand for the book.

Rather than aiming for CEOs, he targeted diversity leaders in corporations. He argued that diversity was the greatest but most overlooked source of innovation in business. Because no one else was making this case, diversity leaders took notice, bought the book, and introduced it to their CEOs, who fell in love with it too.

Demand isn't looking for you. You have to find it. There's a unique angle or audience that will give voice to your cause. It will prime the pump, create social validation, stir the pot, and give people a reason to join your movement.

The greatest achievement was at first and for a time a dream.
The oak sleeps in the acorn.

—JAMES ALLEN

In 2003, when Donald Miller released his second book, *Blue Like Jazz*, he wasn't a popular author. His first book sold a modest 10,000 copies. The second, more of a primer on Christianity for people who felt disenchanted with God, didn't look like it would fare any better. Sales were slow at first. But then the national college ministry Campus Crusade purchased 65,000 copies to place in their

"Freshman Survival Kits" nationwide. It primed the pump. Seeding this audience triggered demand that led to the sale of more than 1.5 million copies. It spent forty-three weeks on the *New York Times* bestseller list.

Demand had been discovered.

The Marketing Plan

Nothing is more deflating than launching a great idea, only to watch it go nowhere. Creating your offering is only half the battle. It requires just as much effort to promote your idea as it does to create it. Hollywood studios spend just as much money to market a film as they do to make it, if that tells you anything.

You need a plan to market your dream.

There's no formula, no rulebook, and no template to follow. In fact, the more unique it is, the easier it will be to differentiate your offering. You also don't need to spend a lot of money. Advertising is great if you have the budget. But a nontraditional approach could help you reach new people, build a grassroots movement, and generate buzz beyond your reach.

A marketing plan isn't just one thing, but many approaches. It could include promotional events, posters, mass e-mails, social media, press releases, webcasts, advertisements, free giveaways, and handwritten notes. You could put out a call for art submissions, a "VIP club" for your best customers, exclusive conference calls, promotional tours, or private Web sites and online communities. The important thing is to identify the activities you can execute well and pursue only those things.

Here's a sample marketing plan that shows how my STORY conference attracts an audience of creative professionals:

- Host creative meet-ups in various cities with free coffee and bagels to connect our audience to one another and the STORY brand.
- Send promotional kits to key influencers.

- Post tweets and Facebook updates to keep our audience engaged and informed throughout the year.
- Send monthly e-mails to our list of contacts with photos, articles, free downloads, and special offers to attend the event.
- Launch a Web site with valuable content and a compelling design in order to attract more visitors to the site.
- Ask more than one hundred bloggers to write posts about the event in exchange for exclusive giveaways or content.
- Promote a sweepstakes to win STORY tickets, airfare, a hotel room, and seats at a Chicago Cubs game in order to grow our mailing list.
- E-mail our list with reminders at each registration deadline to drive sign-ups.
- Exchange ad space with a magazine for exhibit space at our event.
- Ask our event sponsors to promote the event on social media and to their mailing lists as part of our partnership.

This is a small campaign that doesn't cost a lot of money. But it has consistently delivered a sold-out event, which is all we've needed to accomplish. As we grow our event, we'll need to expand the marketing plan in order to reach a larger audience.

You have everything you need to build something far bigger than yourself.

—SETH GODIN

Promoting yourself can be an uncomfortable proposition, but let me put you at ease. This is not about you. It's not about promoting yourself. It's about offering a gift to the world. If you're uncomfortable with it, you've got the wrong idea. Your dream represents something larger than you—the answer to a problem, a wonderful new experience, or a solution to what's lacking in the world.

If you weren't meant to share your dream, it would have been given to someone else. It's your responsibility to steward it and share it with other people.

In February 2012, Dodd Caldwell from Greenville, South Carolina, launched a business called Loft Résumés, which turns ordinary résumés into standout designs from a variety of templates. He generated more than 209,000 page views on his Web site within the first month by carrying out this simple marketing plan:

Week 1: He asked his friends at a coworking space to tweet about his company's launch. Dodd also submitted his Web site to numerous CSS design award sites, which generated lots of page views. There were no sales yet though.

Week 2: Dodd e-mailed a writer at Fast Company Design who had previously covered one of his other businesses to request an article about his new venture. The writer published a piece, which generated more Web traffic and eight orders. Dodd also paid for a Google AdWords campaign, which didn't bring in enough revenue to continue doing it. (You never know until you try.)

Week 3: Dodd reached out to bloggers who appeared on the first page of Google search results under the term "creative résumés." Many of them agreed to write about Loft Résumés in exchange for providing a free giveaway to their readers. At this point, orders started coming in every day.

Week 4: Dodd continued reaching out to bloggers, and sales kept climbing. He found a marketing approach that worked so he leaned into it.

Week 5: Dodd contacted the e-commerce site Fab.com, which offers flash sales, about selling his services. They ran a promotion that lasted seventy-two hours and ended up selling more résumés than Dodd had sold in total up to that point. Additionally, even more bloggers saw the sale on Fab.com and started writing about it as well.

How to Create a Marketing Plan

There's no way to know if your marketing plan will succeed in advance. You make your best guess and then adapt the plan as you discover what works and what doesn't.

Let's walk through the process of putting your plan together:

First, clarify your audience. Write a description of the kind of people you want to reach—their characteristics, their interests, their lifestyle, and so on. Keep in mind that if you try to reach everybody, you'll hit nobody. Aim small, miss small. The more specific you are, the easier it will be to reach them. List all the ways they engage with the world. What magazines do they read? What Web sites do they visit? Where do they shop? What are their preferences and habits? Become an expert on your tribe.

Second, take stock of your resources, such as your budget, your platform, your connections, your team, and your talents. Knowing what tools are at your disposal will help guide the rest of your plan. Can you afford paid advertising? Will your schedule allow you to travel? How many people in your target audience already follow you on social media? Do you have friends who are willing to help?

Third, brainstorm all the ways you could reach your audience. If you can afford advertising, research the costs and demographics of the best outlets. If you have no budget, list all of the free activities you'd consider, including press releases, social media, networking, product samples, and meet-ups. You'll discover what works and what doesn't as you go. Keep your plan in an open hand so you can shift your resources as needed.

Fourth, commission a designer to create the promotional materials for your marketing plan. Give yourself plenty of time to construct the communications arsenal you need.

Finally, plot your marketing plan on a calendar and execute it. Some activities will overlap. Others will be sequential. Some tasks will require customization, such as writing original articles for publications. Others you can automate, such as scheduling tweets by uploading a spreadsheet of content to Sendible.com or HootSuite .com. But plan the work and then work the plan.

Nontraditional Marketing

Marketing isn't just a promotional activity. It's part of your offering. How you come at the world says something about you. It demonstrates your brand's personality. It shapes how people perceive you. And if you do it right, marketing adds value to your offering. It makes your idea even more compelling.

For the past twenty years, the energy drink company Red Bull has bolstered its image by sponsoring extreme sports. They've backed motocross, windsurfing, and cliff-diving events to promote their beverage, but they've also gotten behind ridiculous sports, such as the Flugtag, where people enter homemade flying machines in a competition to plunge off a cliff into water, and a Crashed Ice event in which hockey players race down the icy streets of Quebec.

On October 14, 2012, Red Bull took its marketing efforts to a whole new level. It sponsored base jumper Felix Baumgartner in a feat to leap from a balloon twenty-four miles above the earth, making him the first human to break the sound barrier outside of a motorized vehicle. Felix set the record for the highest manned balloon flight, the highest parachute jump, and the greatest free-fall velocity. Billed as "Red Bull Stratos," the jump was streamed live on YouTube for more than 8 million viewers, generating the most concurrent live-stream views ever.

When they tell me I'm too old to do something, I attempt it immediately.

—PABLO PICASSO

Red Bull's CEO Dietrich Mateschitz wanted to give real meaning to the company's slogan "Red Bull gives you wings." He doesn't believe marketing should be separate from the product. "Since the beginning, it has been a brand philosophy and how to look upon the world, rather than pure marketing for consumer goods," he said.

How can you make marketing an integral part of your brand? What is the personality of your brand and how is that best expressed? Each year on the Fourth of July, more than forty thousand people converge at the corner of Surf and Stillwell avenues in Coney Island to watch Nathan's Famous International Hot Dog Eating Contest. Nathan's isn't just doing it for kicks. They're trying to sell hot dogs.

Nontraditional marketing conveys your message in a way people don't expect and draws them into an experience that conventional approaches could never offer. It's risky. It's not for everyone. And you won't be able to track the results quite so easily. But when nontraditional marketing pays off, it can be powerful.

Here are some approaches to consider:

Transmedia

A transmedia campaign is an interactive experience that leverages multiple media at once. It could be as complex as a national treasure hunt or as simple as a physical product to support your online marketing.

When rap artist Jay-Z's autobiography *Decoded* came out on November 16, 2010, it was no ordinary marketing campaign. But then it was no ordinary book. Jay-Z used the lyrics of his music and corresponding photos to share stories from his life.

Thirty days before its launch, Jay-Z's marketing agency Droga5 placed images of the book's two hundred pages at various locations in thirteen major cities, allowing fans to piece together the book's content before the hardcover hit stores. The locations included a rooftop in New Orleans, a billboard in Chicago, the bottom of a swimming pool in Miami, a boxing gym in Brooklyn, the liner of a jacket at a Gucci store, an LED wall in Times Square, and other sites that correlated to each page's content.

Millions of people flocked to the campaign's Web site for clues to help them find pages and to see how much of the book had already been assembled by fans. *Decoded* stayed on the bestseller lists for nineteen straight weeks and the campaign earned $1.1 billion worth of media impressions.

You're no Jay-Z (yet), but how can you engage people in a trans-media campaign? By asking them to complete tasks, visit relevant locations, interact on multiple platforms, or collaborate with other participants, you're giving people an experience that connects them to your brand.

Meet-ups and Parties

Michael Arrington started the popular technology blog *TechCrunch* in 2005 by throwing parties at his Palo Alto home for movers and shakers in the industry.

Only ten people came to the first one. They grilled hamburgers and drank beer until four in the morning. But the next party drew twenty people; the following one drew one hundred people; then two hundred people. Today, Michael hosts thousands of people at three big events and six smaller ones a year as a way to build buzz and fuel his readership.

Meet-ups and parties aren't meant to be a "hard sell" approach. You may not see a return on your investment right away. But remember that you're building social capital for a bigger "ask" down the road. Plus, you'll have a great time doing it.

Videos

On March 5, 2012, the social justice organization Invisible Children, which works to prevent the recruitment of child soldiers around the world, released a thirty-minute video called *Kony 2012* to bring attention to the Ugandan war criminal Joseph Kony.

Narrated by the organization's CEO Jason Russell, the video sought to "make Kony famous" in order to bring about his arrest. The campaign asked people to lobby twenty "celebrity culture makers," such as Taylor Swift, George Clooney, and Oprah, as well as twelve "policy makers," including George W. Bush, Condoleezza Rice, and John Kerry, to help give voice to the movement. In just seven months, the video was viewed more than 93 million times on YouTube, and surveys showed that nearly half of all American young adults heard about the campaign in the days after it launched. *Time* magazine called it the most viral video of all time.

Invisible Children's video was filmed using consumer-grade cameras and no special effects. It was a simple message with a powerful call to action. There is nothing Invisible Children did that is outside your reach. You only need a video camera, a powerful message, and the resolve to tell your story.

In 2012, Dream Year participant John Finch wanted to capture stories about the impact of fathers on their sons. As a young boy, he survived his own father's suicide and developed a passion to help other men avoid wounding their sons.

John couldn't find a filmmaker who would take on the project. So he bought the equipment, taught himself to use it, traveled across the country on his savings account, and filmed the interviews himself. The videos have generated more than 100,000 views on YouTube, which has enabled John to build a career as an author and speaker through his organization The Perfect Father.

Road Shows

As a kid, I spent my afternoons getting my teeth chipped and shins shredded while practicing tricks on my freestyle BMX. One summer, the famous Hutch Trick Team came through my hometown of Lititz, Pennsylvania, to put on a free demonstration in the local park. They cordoned off an area for spectators and set up ramps for aerial stunts. I remember watching in awe with throngs of other kids as Woody Itson pulled off a no-handed 180 on the halfpipe and showed us how to "surf" by standing on the seat and handlebars. It made me all the more determined to risk teeth and bones in the pursuit of impressing my friends.

Hutch wasn't putting on free shows purely for the entertainment. They wanted to sell more bikes. And it worked. Twenty-five years later, I still have a prized Hutch Trick Star sitting in my closet.

Creating a road show can be as extensive as converting a schoolbus into a mobile showroom like Warby Parker's "Class Trip" or as simple as wrapping a cargo bike with branded graphics like Harry & David to pedal around the neighborhood. A humanitarian organization in San Diego called People of the Second Chance put magnetic signs on a Smart car to turn heads on their tour stops. And my STORY conference restored a 1920s-era hot dog cart to hand out treats to passersby.

Mobile experiences don't always generate revenue right away. But they raise awareness for the brand and make positive investments in prospective customers. People don't always buy something from you in year one. They may come through in year two or three. Marketing is a long game. Think in years, not just days or weeks.

PDF Books

In 2008, entrepreneur Chris Guillebeau released a free PDF book on his blog called *A Brief Guide to World Domination*. The twenty-nine-page manifesto offered a new way of looking at life and career. Chris already had a sizable blog readership, but in just six months, 100,000 people in sixty countries downloaded his manifesto and rallied around his ideas about self-employment, freedom, and traveling the world. It spawned a physical book called *The Art of Non-Conformity*, a sold-out conference in Portland called the World Domination Summit, and a follow-up book entitled *The $100 Startup*.

Offering a PDF book on a specific topic is a great way to build your mailing list, grow your expertise, and draw attention to your dream. Call it a "manifesto," a "white paper," or an "e-book"— you're giving people a way to follow you and spread your ideas. After you write the book—it doesn't have to be long—hire a designer to format it and then make it available in exchange for contact information. You can keep building your tribe by sending ongoing content or follow-up offers.

Value-Added Experiences

When the movie *Looper* starring Bruce Willis came out in 2012, the writer and director Rian Johnson provided a downloadable MP3 audio commentary on his blog for viewers to listen to while watching the film in theaters. He instructed them to use headphones, dim the screens on their devices, and only listen to it on the second viewing. It created additional buzz and compelled fans to see the film twice so they could hear the director's commentary along with the action.

How can you add value to your current offering as a way to build buzz? What about offering a "concierge service" to your most frequent customers? A business conference in Atlanta called Leadercast offers complimentary dry cleaning to attendees during the event. What if you kept some offerings hidden to everyone but your most devoted fans? It's rumored that the restaurant chain Chipotle has a "secret menu" that only its most passionate customers know about.

Publicity Stunts

In 2009, the Queensland tourism agency in Australia conducted a publicity stunt to attract more visitors to the Great Barrier Reef. They placed advertisements in national newspapers offering "The World's Best Job" at $150,000 to the best-qualified applicant who would take care of Hamilton Island.

The winning candidate would stay on the island for six months, blog about his or her experience, and spend the rest of the time driving around in a golf cart, enjoying the sunshine, swimming, and surfing. It wasn't a real job, of course. It was a publicity stunt to promote the island as a tourist destination. But it made one hell of a story.

The campaign generated $89 million worth of publicity and attracted 35,000 applicants. A thirty-four-year-old British charity worker named Ben Southall got the job.

The trick is to flip the "value proposition" from always wanting something from your customers to offering them something of surprising value. Tourism Queensland already had the bungalow, the golf cart, and the marketing budget. All they did was frame these assets into the job of a lifetime. It wasn't really a job, but they got more publicity this way than by describing it as a sweepstakes.

What assets, abilities, or relationships do you have that could be reframed into something buzzworthy? Start with the dream scenarios that your customers wish for.

Contests

In 2011, Canon partnered with filmmaker Ron Howard to host a contest called Project Imagin8ion that invited photographers to submit images based on eight movie-related categories: setting, character, mood, time, goal, relationship, obstacle, and the unknown. Out of 96,362 submissions, Ron selected eight winning photos that would inspire a screenplay for a short film called *When You Find Me*.

The film was directed by Ron's daughter Bryce and shot entirely with Canon gear. It premiered at the Sundance, Tribeca, and SXSW film festivals, where the contest's winners accompanied Ron and Bryce on the red carpet.

Contests not only get people talking about your brand but help them become emotionally invested as well. People care more about your cause when they're able to contribute in some way. It helps them feel like they're part of what you're doing. Make your logo assets available for a design contest. Call for photo submissions using a hashtag on Instagram. Reward the best solution to a problem.

You want people to have a sense of ownership in your brand. It will remain a small dream if you keep it to yourself. The writer Charles Brower said, "Few people are successful unless a lot of other people want them to be." Plus, if you retain ownership or usage rights of the contributions, you end up with assets you can leverage for your brand. Make sure you talk to an attorney before sponsoring a contest so you don't run into legal issues later on.

Promotional Kits

In 2012, the advertising agency Wieden+Kennedy created promotional kits for the animated film *ParaNorman* that generated plenty of online buzz. It shipped large wooden boxes labeled "Blithe Hollow Cemetery" with no other instructions to leading entertainment bloggers.

Upon opening the box, the recipients discovered a tiny shovel lying on top of sod-covered dirt. Under the surface was a tiny coffin with a character from the film lying inside and the date of his demise. Each character held a rolled-up paper with a hand-scribed note to the recipient and a miniature movie poster. If the bloggers continued to sift through the dirt, they found tiny burlap bags filled with candy, a tiny manila folder, a parking cone, a sewer inspection certificate, and other items from the movie. Without exception, the bloggers posted photos and videos of the box on their sites.

No doubt, Wieden+Kennedy spent a lot of money on these "influencer kits," but they're easy to create for less. In 2010, my STORY conference sent fifty promotional kits to influential bloggers for about $40 each. As a way to reinforce our theme of storytelling, we purchased fake book boxes at a home decorator's clearance sale. Inside, we placed a tobacco pipe, a rolled-up event poster, three books from our presenters, a handwritten note from me, and a "mix tape" USB device with free resources. All of the recipients blogged about their experience of opening the box, which generated tens of thousands of Web impressions for our brand.

Make the Most of Your Launch

You only get one chance to launch your dream before it becomes just another project that once was. Real estate loses value the longer it sits on the market. New cars lose value the instant they're driven off the lot. The same is true of your dream. You don't have long to present a new idea to the world before it enters the land of has-beens. So let's make the most of it. Here's how:

First, prepare for the duration of your campaign. If you're launching a book, you need a solid year to promote it. If you're launching an event, it takes at least six months to build an audience. Every dream is different, so figure out how much time your campaign requires and prepare for the sprint. Come out of the gate strong, but identify the milestones you need to hit along the way.

For example, not everyone signs up for a conference the moment it's announced. So organizers create deadlines that motivate people to register at price increases leading up to the event. You can do the same with limited-time offers, monthly packages, or special incentives. This way, you create multiple reasons to contact your audience throughout the year and surges of revenue along the way.

Second, use every tool in your arsenal to launch your dream. Ask your friends for help. Leverage your connections. Call in favors. And keep the pressure on yourself to achieve what you never have before. Launching your dream might be the most challenging undertaking of your life, but it's worth it. You can endure almost anything for a season.

In Dream Year, most people launch projects while working full-time jobs. I recommend taking a few days off when your project launches to do the necessary work of promoting your dream. It takes a lot of personal e-mails, calls, and tweets to get people talking.

Third, get momentum on your side. Momentum doesn't come from waiting for big breaks. You create momentum by accomplishing small wins along the way. Every bit of publicity, every retweet and "like," every opened e-mail, and every accepted invitation is something to work for and celebrate.

What we think, or what we know, or what we believe is, in the end, of little consequence. The only consequence is what we do.

—JOHN RUSKIN

Opportunities don't happen until you take action. That's the formula. You act and then things happen. Sometimes they're not even correlated. But this is the mysterious way of dream chasing. Action opens doors.

Fourth, make big asks of people who can help. Launching your dream is one of the most important things you'll ever do. It's worth the discomfort of putting yourself out there. Ask your friends to share it with *their* friends. Ask someone to be your first customer. Ask for publicity. Ask for meetings. Ask other entrepreneurs how they did it. You will get rejected, and your skin will grow thick. But other people will say yes, and it will all be worth it. Good things happen when you start making asks.

Measure Your Marketing

As you carry out your marketing plan, the goal is to move from what doesn't work to the things that do, from a shotgun-blast approach to precision sharpshooting. There is a way that works. But you have to try a variety of methods to find it.

Measure your marketing. Behind every successful idea is a real and calculable method for gaining customers. Marketing is only mysterious when you fail to keep track of the results.

As an event organizer, I've learned that registration deadlines motivate attendees to sign up even more than the prices do. In other words, it's not the cost savings that drive people to sign up as much as the date itself. For example, if we set a registration deadline on the 15th of the month, there will not only be a surge of sign-ups on the 15th but on the 30th as well, because people assume that the end of the month is an important date. So each year, after the 15th has passed, our team promotes the 30th as an important date to register (for no real reason at all), and we get two surges in one month.

The numbers don't lie.

In 2009, Christian Rudder, cofounder of the dating site OkCupid, took his users' data and looked for interesting results. He kept the participants anonymous, but as a Harvard-educated mathematician, Christian couldn't help but analyze the data. With information from more than a million people at his disposal, he discovered the best poses for profile pictures (men should look away from the camera; women should make a "flirty face"). And users should avoid using physical compliments in their initial messages. If there's a science behind finding a date, there's certainly one behind your marketing.

Think of your marketing plan as a series of experiments. Track the results from everything you do. You can track social media results with online tools, but for anything offline, ask your customers how they heard about you. Discard what doesn't work and double down on the things that do. Marketing doesn't have to be a mystery. It's a puzzle to be solved. With enough measured experimentation, you'll find the best way to promote your dream.

Look for the Lights in Their Living Rooms

In 1956, Jerry Falwell started a church in his hometown of Lynchburg, Virginia. He knocked on a hundred doors a day to invite people to attend his services. But as he walked through the neighborhoods at night hoping to catch people on their front porches, he noticed a phenomenon that changed his approach to ministry.

He noticed the lights in their living rooms.

It seemed that every family was gathered around a glowing television set after dinner for evening entertainment. He found people anxious to end the conversation and get back to watching TV. Not one to be ignored, Jerry resolved to go where people were already gathered. He started his own television ministry and became one of the first televangelists in history.

Most of us beat our heads against the wall trying to bring our dreams to life. We try the proven marketing methods, but people seem distracted by other things.

Look for the lights in their living rooms. Watch how your target audience spends its time and adjust your marketing efforts to meet them there.

If they're teenagers, try a Snapchat account. If they're pet owners, try a mobile cart at dog parks. If they're mothers of small children, there are only certain hours in the day when you can engage them. You have to meet them where they're at.

When the room-sharing site Airbnb was getting off the ground in 2008, the founders Brian Chesky and Joe Gebbia went door to door in New York to recruit new users. When Ben Silbermann launched the photo-sharing site Pinterest in 2010, he noticed that many of its early users were interested in design, so he went to a conference for design bloggers to recruit more users.

This Year's Offering Is Next Year's Marketing

You have to promote your offering. There's no getting around that. But it's not your only option. This year's offering is next year's marketing.

In the early years of my STORY conference, we intentionally capped the attendance in order to sell out the event in advance. It pained me to say no to other people who came along (and the additional revenue). But by giving up short-term revenue, we boosted demand for the next year's sales.

The conventional thinking in marketing is to launch large and make an immediate return on investment. But people don't want what's available to them in abundance. It undermines demand. Attractive brands are exclusive. In many cases, launching small with high quality contributes to your future success. Sure, you'll miss out on short-term revenue, but the long-term benefits are worth it.

Jason Locy is a talented designer who runs a boutique studio in Atlanta called FiveStone. He creates mind-blowing projects for Chick-fil-A, MTV, and other national organizations. When I asked him whether he was looking for new clients, he said he had all the work he could handle. There was no need for him to promote himself. His work spoke for itself. He had gotten to the place where his unavailability created even more demand for his services. He could pick and choose his clients.

This is where you want to be.

You want people to want to work with you. You don't want to be making cold calls and offering discounted prices, practically begging people to hire you. You want customers to call *you*. You want to be able to say no to the projects you don't want and yes to the ones you do. You want to be able to charge premium prices. And the only way to do that is to control your growth—to make this year's offering so special, so exclusive, and so in-demand that it enhances next year's offering.

My brother- and sister-in-law Drs. Lou and Tiffany Fernandez opened a chiropractic office in Virginia Beach, Virginia, a few years ago. To fill their appointment schedule in the early months, they could have broadcast their availability. But knowing that it would undermine demand, we tried a more exclusive approach. They announced on their Facebook page that three select appointments were open on, say, Thursday to the first people who responded. Without fail, patients scrambled to secure the spots, and everyone else was directed to appointments at other times during the week.

Being unavailable made them all the more popular.

The Trouble with Free

There's a dangerous misconception that if people could only experience what we have to offer for free, they might be willing to pay for the next one.

In theory, people like free.

Chris Anderson's book *Free* tells us it's the business strategy of the future. Stores can give away free products by charging manufacturers shelf-space fees. Record labels can give away music by distributing it through no-cost, digital channels. Organizations are getting creative at finding alternative ways to generate revenue.

The trouble is, people don't buy it.

While we enthusiastically embrace the idea of free, we treat it with very little respect. Free carries with it an inherent perception of no value.

In October 2012, psychologists Kimberlee Weaver, Stephen Garcia, and Norbert Schwarz proved this notion in a series of consumer studies. When they presented buyers with a choice between a package that included an iPod, an iPod cover, and one free song download and a package that included just an iPod and cover, consumers were willing to pay an average of $177 for the package *with* the download and $242 for the one *without* the download.

In other words, the more you value your own offerings, the more other people will. Of course, consumers will tell you that free give-aways add more value. But their actions disagree.

I once spoke with the veteran sales leader of a conference organization that specialized in leadership events. She had spent more than ten years selling conference registrations and learned a very important lesson: never give away free tickets. After opening her heart and giving free tickets to numerous people who said they couldn't afford the event, she discovered that they would almost never show up. It didn't matter how much they begged or pleaded on the phone about their difficult circumstances. At the end of the day, they didn't value free.

Exclusivity is, unfortunately, an effective marketing strategy. We want what we can't have. Even more, we want what other people can't have, and we're willing to pay good money to keep it that way. Exclusivity is expensive, but we value it more. We tell ourselves it's more meaningful, that we're better for it.

Free is too unsophisticated for our palates. We ask ourselves, "How could anything truly valuable be free?" When I'm waiting in line at Starbucks, I routinely ignore the free iTunes "Pick of the Week" cards, because how could free music be any good? Never mind that it's Sting.

Even Facebook, which is free to everyone, got started under exclusive conditions. Not only did the first users have to be in college, they had to attend Harvard. And not only did they have to attend Harvard, they had to be a part of the Phoenix "Final Club," one of the school's secret societies. From there, Facebook spread to other Ivy League colleges before being released to other universities, high schools, and finally the general public. There's no doubt that Facebook's limited release contributed to its rapid growth. We all want what we can't have.

Fake It Until You Make It

In the late 1970s, a little-known band from Dublin, Ireland, called U2 was struggling to make it in the music business. They were a hometown favorite in local bars, but in order to get a record deal, they needed to play in a bigger city. Dublin wasn't big enough.

So the four members—Bono, Adam Clayton, Larry Mullen, Jr., and The Edge—borrowed money from their parents and embarked on a trip to London, which, according to Bono, scared them all to death. It was an overwhelming city with seedy venues that drew too few people. But London was the only place the band could get signed. So they borrowed just enough money from their parents for a weeklong tour. They managed to get booked for a few shows and invited some record producers to attend.

In the book *U2 by U2*, Bono recounted their experience:

"On that tour they were going to decide whether to sign us or not. This was a make-it or break-it situation. On the good nights they didn't show up, on the bad nights they did. At the end of the week, all the record companies had passed on us. . . . We ended up going home red-faced, without the recording deal that we'd promised our fans and fathers."

U2 had spent all of their money and blown their one chance to make it in London. They had no other choice but to go home to Dublin and keep playing music in local bars.

That is, of course, unless they faked their success.

"We had one last idea," Bono explained, "which was based on the sense that the Irish press has a history of colluding with Irish people who cause a bit of a stir in the outside world, and fanning those little sparks into a forest fire. We started to work on the concept of U2 breaking the UK."

In other words, U2 decided to pretend they had made it big in London by feeding impressions to the Irish press. They weren't lying. They simply managed people's perceptions. Dublin was 362 miles away. They'd never know the reality.

"So forget about playing third on the bill to 10 people," Bono said. "The way we were telling it, 200 people turned up to see us in the Half Moon in Herne Hill. We then booked an Irish tour, which climaxed at the National Stadium in Dublin, which no junior act had ever done before. It was a place that only the greats played, the boxing stadium in Dublin. And people were aghast. 'Have U2 really broken that big? Yes, they're that big. They are!' "

The way to being taken seriously is to act seriously. In other words, fake it until you make it. Seth Godin explains in *The Dip* that people don't have a lot of time to explore options and don't want to take a lot of risks, so they narrow their choices to a few winning contenders. "Faced with an infinite number of choices," he writes, "many people pick the market leader." If you're not the market leader and hope to have any shot at becoming one, you have to make people think you already are.

I refuse to recognize that there are impossibilities. I cannot discover that anyone knows enough about anything on this earth definitely to say what is and what is not possible.

—HENRY FORD

The Edge explained what happened to U2: "Just having gone to London was almost as good as having a record deal in people's eyes."

The way to be taken seriously is to start acting seriously. Represent your brand with the finest design you can afford. Amplify the moments that bolster your image. Partner with larger brands. Recruit clients that elevate your standing. Make the most of every opportunity. And celebrate wins so that other people can celebrate too. If you believe in your dream's potential, they'll start to believe it too.

Call to Action

Marketing is the act of creating demand for your dream. If you've designed an idea model that solves a problem and provides a unique offering that people want, you've been doing the work of marketing all this time. If no one is buying what you're selling, it's critical to revisit the idea model. Tweak the formula until you come up with an offering that people crave. Otherwise, selling will be tough.

Once you've determined the best idea model, you need a great marketing plan. This is a list of activities that will launch your idea to the world. It can include conventional outlets such as magazine ads, press releases, and direct mail, but don't overlook unconventional approaches such as social media, transmedia experiences, live events, parties, open houses, and word of mouth.

Here's your assignment at this stage of Dream Year: Create a marketing plan for your dream. List all of the ways you'll launch your dream to the world.

QUESTIONS:

1. What is the level of demand for your offering right now? What can you do to increase it?
2. What cues are giving away your weakness in the market? How can you better manage perceptions of your project or organization?
3. What does a market leader look like in your field? What are the telltale signs? How can you start acting like one? Fake it until you make it.

10

GROWING
THE BUSINESS

**Whenever you see a successful business, someone once
made a courageous decision.**

....

—PETER DRUCKER

Turning a Dream into a Business

Dream Year is about doing what you love and making a unique
contribution to the world. But it's not meant to be a hobby. The goal
is to create income so you can afford to keep doing it, benefit other
people, and earn a good living, maybe even a great one. You
accomplish this by identifying how the dream creates revenue,
ensuring that the revenue is greater than your expenses, and then
maximizing that formula for the benefit of all. In other words, you
turn it into a business.

Sure, you can keep doing it as a hobby. You can continue squeez-
ing it into the margins of your life. You can have an on-again, off-
again relationship with your dream where you pursue it only when
you feel like it or as your schedule permits.

But if your dream provides a gift to the world and satisfies a great
purpose within you, you're going to stay in a perpetual state of frustration. As a hobbyist, you'll always struggle with cash flow, your
impact will be small, and it will be like starting from scratch each
time you endeavor to do it.

I realize you can't quit your job right away. You've got bills to pay, mouths to feed, and a future to protect. But you can identify your number—the amount of money it would take to replace your salary, your health insurance, and the cost of going into business. You may have to cut out lattes or kill cable TV or downgrade your car to make it manageable. But you can calculate the number of consulting sessions or e-books or conference registrations you need to sell each month to replace your salary.

Then you can start working in the margins of your life—the late nights and early mornings—to make it a full-time reality. You'll work harder than you've ever worked before. But this is your one chance to break free from the cubicle and find the revenue model in your dream.

I understand the reluctance. It took me ten years of false starts to build up the courage to follow my dream once and for all. When you're starting a business, people don't exactly line up to encourage you. Your relatives think you're irresponsible, your friends think you're crazy, your colleagues don't understand what you're doing, and your boss does everything she can to dissuade you.

The world doesn't like an outlier.

But it's worth it.

Your business doesn't need to have employees. It doesn't have to be large. It doesn't even need to be incorporated. But it does need a formal structure so it can grow, build momentum, become self-sustaining, and serve people well.

You don't even have to run it. Recruit a team of capable people who can do that for you if needed. Or sell it. You were appointed to birth the dream, not necessarily to manage it. But turning it into a business is the summit to which all dreamers must climb. Otherwise, you'll make no lasting impact.

Higher-Yielding Results

Dream Year participant Bryan Allain once described the plight of dreamers who start something while working full-time jobs: "We use 60 percent of our capacity at work because of our dreams. But we can only give 60 percent of our capacity to the dream because of our work. As a result, we operate at 120 percent of our capacity, and it's exhausting."

When you're working hard at a dream that's yielding too few results, it's inevitable—you're going to run out of energy and quit. The solution is to produce "higher-yielding results." Find a way to create more revenue without putting in more time.

There are two ways to do this:

Increase your customers, or increase your profit.

To increase your customers without adding more time to your work, your offering has to be scalable. In other words, you have to sell something *other than* your time. For example, whether I attract five hundred people or a thousand people to my events, I'm doing the exact same thing for them. No additional time is needed for each attendee. I only need more seats. But if I increase the number of consulting clients I serve, each one adds more time to my schedule. I'm limited by how many clients I can take on. One activity is scalable. The other is not.

Can your dream be scaled to more customers or donors without requiring more of your time?

Carolyn Jewel is the author of more than twenty historical and paranormal romance novels that were released by various publishers over the years. Many of them had gone out of print, and the publishers stopped releasing them. Rather than writing more novels, Carolyn recovered the rights to her backlisted titles and is rereleasing them as e-books for Kindle, iPad, and Nook.

"In six weeks, I've made three times the advance I was paid initially," she said. Carolyn found a way to sell more books without writing new ones.

Maybe your work could be automated so it doesn't require your time at all.

Mica May from Houston came to our 2010 Dream Year weekend in Nashville to improve her business, which makes beautiful, custom-monogrammed journals called May Books. Until then, Mica processed every order by hand. She took the order to a printer, then took the printed sheets to a stitching company for binding, and finally shipped the books herself. On top of all this, she added a handwritten note to thank customers for their purchases. It was a time-consuming process to say the least.

Motivated to scale her business, Mica found a printing company that would automatically print, stitch, and ship each order in one fell swoop. In fact, the printing company even purchased additional equipment so it could handle all of Mica's business. As a result, Mica never even sees the journals anymore. She figured out how to scale her dream to reach more customers, while at the same time freeing up more time in her schedule to market the products and grow her business.

The other way to create higher-yielding results is to increase your profits. You can do this by raising prices or cutting costs. If you've got strong demand for your offerings or need higher paying clients, you may need to increase your prices. In 2010, Dream Year participant Kate Schmidgall made a bold decision to double the fee she was charging clients for graphic design. She lost some customers at first, but she gained better ones and has become far more profitable with the same amount of work.

Cutting costs involves taking a hard look at your expenses and figuring out how to reduce or eliminate them. If you can't do either one, you can always create a new idea model, something with a better profit margin. Remember, you're not the employee who has to accept working conditions the way they are anymore. As the CEO, you get to design the business.

Bryan was facing "dream fatigue" when he talked about the 120 percent capacity problem. He was coaching a modest number of clients for a modest amount of revenue on top of his already-busy life as a father, husband, and full-time engineer. He wasn't getting anywhere at this rate. So he decided to launch a whole new offering— a conference for bloggers. He could charge more money per person and scale his knowledge to more people without adding more time to his schedule. The strategy worked. One year later, Bryan quit his job to focus on his dream full-time.

If you're getting worn out and aren't making enough money to justify the effort, you don't have a capacity problem. You have a formula problem.

Let's explore some ideas.

You could sell yearlong "memberships" instead of "one-off" purchases. You could host workshops for groups instead of consulting people one-on-one. You could recruit freelancers instead of doing all the work yourself so you can spend more time on tasks that actually grow the business.

Remember, a great idea is a spreadsheet with skin on. It has to be profitable. It has to fit your capacity. Otherwise, you'll burn out and quit.

And that's no good for anyone.

Sarah Bray from Virginia Beach, Virginia, ran a graphic design studio called S.Joy Studios for several years. She cranked out logo after logo, Web site after Web site, and campaign after campaign to the satisfaction of her clients. But it was a busy life, a life with too little significance for her taste. Sure, it was profitable, but her revenue depended on her workload. The more time she spent, the more money she made. But it had no impact on whether the client's business succeeded or failed because she wasn't hired to speak into the product itself.

As a mother, a writer, and an otherwise introspective person with dreams and passions of her own, Sarah didn't want this kind of life. So she closed the studio as she knew it and came up with an entirely new offering called A Small Nation.

It was more than a design studio. It was a new way of doing business that would help clients create a holistic plan for building a loyal customer base—a small nation. Graphic design would be part of her offerings but only a small part. Sarah said, "Marketing isn't about building a fancy Web site or getting your name out to as many people as possible. It starts with the concept of what you are doing and why. You have to believe in what you're doing before you can get other people to believe it with you, and you have to be able to design and communicate around it so that your heart comes across."

Sarah envisioned an entirely new way of building a business. It needed to grow out of purpose, meaning, and story. She would help clients structure their offerings first and then and only then create their branding. And she would only accept a few select clients she truly believed in each year at a higher price point. This was the kind of life and work that Sarah imagined for herself.

"I was convinced that if I was allowed to work in the most perfect way possible, then my work would be the best it's ever been," she said.

If you've launched your dream but aren't experiencing a life you love, you've put down the tools too soon. There is still work to do on your model. It was never going to happen in one attempt anyway. It's a series of steps you must take to discard the things you don't like and pursue the things you do.

Ways to Grow Your Business

By now, the faucet of revenue on your dream should be dripping so that at least you know there's water in the well. The goal is to get the faucet gushing so your dream can take off. This doesn't come from having epiphanies. It comes from trial and error, tweaking the model, and turning the tumblers of your idea until it finally clicks. Once it does, here are some ways to grow the business:

Adjust Your Idea Model

If your idea model isn't working, change it. People aren't interested in blah upstarts with blah offerings that compete with other blah businesses. Your idea needs to stand apart and offer something surprisingly good. Besides, as your idea thrives and spreads, it won't be long before someone else copies your model. If you don't stay ahead of the competition, they'll overtake you in no time.

In 1997, the founder of Netflix, Reed Hastings, revolutionized the video rental industry by offering DVDs by mail in returnable envelopes. His ingenuity and forward thinking knocked Blockbuster off its high horse.

But in 2010, when Blockbuster adopted a home delivery service and started nipping at his company's heels, Reed changed the model once again by offering streaming movies online. He created the idea that would put his own DVD mailing service out of business before someone else did.

As the competition and costs for movie rights increased, Reed decided to make television shows, not films, the main source of streaming content for Netflix. While some customers complained about the lack of movies, Netflix saw the average subscriber consuming over an hour's worth of content every single day. It's helped the company reach more than 40 million subscribers as of November 2013.

But TV studios didn't enjoy giving up so much revenue and started raising prices on Netflix. So Reed disrupted his model yet again by creating his own original content with shows such as *Lilyhammer*, *House of Cards*, and *Orange Is the New Black*. Each of them cost up to $100 million to make, but that's far less than the billions of dollars Netflix spent on licensing content from other studios. Reed said the company would spend as much as 15 percent of its budget on creating original content in the future.

How can you improve your own model before your competitors do? On an episode of the TV series *Shark Tank*, entrepreneur Mark Cuban said, "I ask myself, 'If I was going to kick my own ass, what would I do?'" This is your challenge—to figure out how you would beat yourself at your own game and then go and do that. Starting your own business isn't a place where you arrive and stay comfortable. It's a continual process of innovation, experimentation, and change.

Quit What Doesn't Work

Every system is perfectly designed to achieve the results that it gets. So if you're not getting good results, quit doing it. America Online knows this better than anyone. At one time, AOL was the primary gateway to the Internet. It made Web browsing easy and accessible to anyone with a dial-up account. But with the advent of broadband, cable, and DSL Internet connections, AOL has become, quite frankly, unnecessary.

Not everyone figured this out, however, which is why AOL is still in business. The company gets most of its revenue from elderly people who have high-speed Internet service but fail to realize they don't need to keep paying $25 a month to access the Web.

A former AOL executive said, "The dirty little secret is that seventy-five percent of the people who subscribe to AOL's dial-up service don't need it."

For as many people who are in the dark about this, many more people *have* figured it out. In 2002, the company had 35 million subscribers. Today, AOL has only 2.58 million, and the numbers keep declining.

So AOL's CEO, Tim Armstrong, is changing the system. He's turning the company into a local news service. Thanks to its years as the reigning Internet portal, AOL's home page still receives more than 36 million unique users every month. With this amount of traffic as a foundation, Tim is shifting the company into a journalism business that reports local news and filters the best of the Web.

If people aren't buying what you have to offer, it means they don't want it. So how can you shift your offering into something people value? It may only need a few small tweaks. It might require a complete overhaul. But it all starts with your willingness to quit what doesn't work and find the thing that does.

Find Great Partners

When Dream Year's John Finch completed his documentary film about the need for better fathers, he was thrilled to get 100,000 views on YouTube but needed a bigger partner to help spread the film's message. Knowing that psychologists and counselors were invested in the topic of fatherhood but lacked helpful media resources, John approached the American Association of Christian Counselors about licensing the film. With more than fifty thousand members worldwide, a publishing company, and countless events, the AACC signed an agreement with John in November 2013 to distribute the film along with a new small group curriculum and a book about John's life.

As you seek to find partners for your dream, think about your offering from someone else's perspective. What can you offer them in exchange for the value you need? Even if you're the smaller organization and have much more to gain from the partnership than they do, there's something of immense value you can offer them. Look for a win-win scenario and make the big ask.

Create New Offerings

Your business can grow by adding new offerings that leverage the momentum you've gained in another core area. This is how best-selling books get turned into movies, best-selling movies get turned into product lines, and best-selling product lines get turned into retail stores. When you add new offerings, you give people more ways to experience your brand.

In September 2012, recording artist Michael Neale released his first novel, *The River*, which tells the story of a young boy whose father died in a whitewater-rafting trip on the Colorado River and who seeks closure by visiting the site as a teenager. As a musician Michael produced a live musical and narrative performance of the story that he toured in theaters and churches for additional exposure and income. Several teachers attended a performance in Palm Beach Gardens, Florida, and approached him to find out how multimedia experiences could enhance reading in the classroom. Michael is now working with them to develop a conference that shows educators how schools can bring stories to life.

What new offerings can you add to grow your business model?

Deliver It Differently

Burger King has been doing business pretty much the same way since the 1950s. It opens fast-food restaurants in shopping malls, freestanding stores, and airports where you can "have it your way" with hamburgers and french fries. But in 2012, the company quietly tested home delivery in the greater Washington, D.C., area to see if it would work. The company even developed its own thermal packaging to keep the food hot on delivery runs. The experiment was so successful that Burger King has expanded the service to fifteen other cities as of this writing. If it can do for hamburgers what delivery did for the pizza industry, it could be a game changer.

How can you deliver your idea in a new and interesting way? Just because you developed an idea for one context doesn't mean you can't repurpose it for others. What about a video version of your e-book; a downloadable product, rather than a physical one; or an online version of your actual course? If you find yourself resisting new expressions of your industry, you might be onto something. Every new advancement feels like you're breaking a rule at first. The best ideas leave your competitors crying, "You're not allowed to do that!" but then asking themselves, "Why didn't we think of that?"

Expand Your Territory

As an event organizer, I can tell you that no matter how "national" an event tries to be, it can't help but be regional. Most people are willing to travel only so far to be part of a conference. So if you want it to grow larger, you have to expand to other parts of the country. My STORY conference has explored the idea of launching "simulcast lounges" in other cities that provide a comfortable space for locals to watch our mainstage talks via high-definition streaming video at a lower price point.

But expanding your business is not just about geography. New territory can include "sidesteps" into relevant industries. When Chipotle Mexican Grill opened in Denver in 1993, it offered a simple menu of make-your-own burritos and tacos. Over the past decade, Chipotle has grown to 1,500 stores in forty-three states with a rocketing stock value. It's clearly a formula that works.

To expand its business, Chipotle not only added stores, it also sidestepped into a new category of food. In 2011, it opened a test store in Washington, D.C., called ShopHouse Southeast Asian Kitchen, which features an Asian twist on the same Chipotle formula. Instead of burritos and tacos, ShopHouse offers bowls of beef, pork, chicken, or tofu, served with your choice of vegetables, toppings, and sauces. The formula is the same. But it's a whole new category of food.

In December 2013, Chipotle announced that it was expanding the formula to make-your-own pizza with the acquisition of Pizzeria Locale in Denver.

What are you doing well? What formula works for you? Now how can you sidestep into new territories with that formula? It might be geographical, but it could also be a new category or industry.

Go "Open Source"

Sebastian Thrun is a computer science professor at Stanford University who also works for Google developing driverless cars and robots. He was frustrated that his artificial intelligence class at Stanford attracted only 200 students, so he decided to offer an online version to anyone who wanted to sign up at a cost of $1. By the start of the course, more than 160,000 people had signed up. Rather than boring the students with video lectures, Sebastian posed problems for the students to solve in one class and discussed solutions in the next one. Twenty-three thousand students finished the course, with the highest-scoring Stanford student placing 411th. Sebastian set up his own company called Udacity to continue exploring how education as a whole can be open-sourced.

Don't be afraid to open your formula to other people for customization. Threadless in Chicago has built a solid business on letting customers design the T-shirts that are sold in their stores. It feels like you're giving away the secret recipe, but customers demonstrate a remarkable loyalty to companies that trust them with their assets. Just look at Wikipedia.

Call to Action

It's okay to have hobbies, but Dream Year is designed to turn your idea into a growing business. Once you have a working idea model that's generating income, it's time to grow your operations.

The first thing to do is turn the tumblers. Like a chiropractor whose job is to align the human body so it can function properly, your job is to align the systems of your dream to make the most of it. Maybe you're charging too little. Or maybe you're charging too much. Maybe you're promoting one package when you should be highlighting another. Maybe you need more "levels of engagement." Maybe your company needs to narrow its focus or change its name. Never stop searching for the right combination of factors that will crack the code and unlock your potential.

Second, look for ways to generate higher-yielding results. Too many dreamers launch ideas with meager earning potential and do nothing about it. Their dream becomes just another job that pays them less than what they could make working for someone else. Consider raising prices or contracting another person to increase your organization's capacity. Think about ways you can automate your process so that you're doing less work for more money. List all the ways that come to mind.

Finally, identify a few ways you can expand or grow your business. Come up with a game plan to kick your own ass. What would you do if you were your competitor and wanted to beat you? Once you've come up with it, go out and do it.

QUESTIONS:

1. How has your dream proved to be successful so far? What are the early indicators of success upon which you can build?
2. If your idea isn't becoming all that it could be, adapt the model. What "tumblers" can you turn to improve your idea

model? What are some ways you can generate higher-yielding results?

3. How could thinking about your dream in "versions" help you succeed? What tumbler do you think is currently not working?

11

SUSTAINING THE DREAM

You wait and watch and work: you don't give up.
....
—ANNE LAMOTT

Don't Quit

You were lured into your dream by the glamour of a realized vision. But you probably didn't count on the setbacks, disappointments, and shortfalls along the way. If you haven't thought about quitting by now, you are most certainly the first person in the history of dreaming. Heartache and discouragement are par for the course.

But I've learned something from watching countless people go after their dreams, only to hit a brick wall and give up. When they quit, it's not usually because they ran out of money or faced an insurmountable obstacle. It's because they were mentally defeated. They believed failure was imminent, and the worry, fear, and pressure all became too much for them to bear.

But in most cases, the failure never actually happened.

The humorist Don Herold once said, "If I had my life to live over, I would perhaps have more actual troubles but I'd have fewer imaginary ones." It is these imaginary failures that plague us the most. We quit because we *might* run out of money. We give up because we *might* fail. We walk away because it *might* flop. Many of us go through life with one hand on the rip cord, looking for any reason to pull it. But the secret to accomplishing your dream is to sabotage the backup plan. If walking away is an option, you and I will take it each and every time the dream gets difficult.

I remember trying out for the high school basketball team when I was in the ninth grade. I had already been running for several months to condition myself, but I wasn't prepared for the level of intensity that my coach had in store for me. He made me run harder and faster than I had ever run before in my life. I remember gasping for breath on every lap, my sides aching from the pain, the nausea, and the feeling of wanting to vomit. I thought I was going to die.

One thing was for sure—I was never coming back.

But the next day at school, I was surprised to learn that none of my teammates were quitting. No one had staged a protest at our harsh treatment. In fact, they weren't even complaining. They viewed the conditioning as a sort of initiation. They seemed proud of it. To preserve my dignity, I had no choice but to go back the next day. And do you know what? I survived. And I survived the next day. And the day after that. Pretty soon, I was not only conditioned to my coach's expectations; I actually loved running at this level. It made me a better athlete.

It's hard to beat a person who never gives up.

—BABE RUTH

Quitting is not always wrong. If the strain is too much for you to bear, by all means, walk away. But you have to establish the conditions for quitting long before you experience the hardship. You have to give your will a chance to stand up to your whim.

In Seth Godin's book *The Dip*, he describes how ultramarathoner Dick Collins perseveres through difficult races:

"Decide before the race the conditions that will cause you to stop and drop out. You don't want to be out there saying, 'Well gee, my leg hurts, I'm a little dehydrated, I'm sleepy, I'm tired, and it's cold and windy' and talk yourself into quitting. If you are making a decision based on how you feel at that moment, you will probably make the wrong decision."

You have to do the same thing when it comes to your dream. You have to draw lines in the sand. What are your conditions for quitting? Decide now before you go any further so that when times get hard (and they will get hard), you can persevere through them. Without knowing your true limitations, you'll be tempted to quit at every heartache and setback you encounter.

Once when I was despairing over the loss of $15,000 on a personal project, I wrote to my friend Tony and confessed that I wanted to quit. He sent me this e-mail:

"Ben, I'm reminded of a documentary I once watched about NASA sending probes to Mars. The head of all things Mars at NASA said something that struck me. He said that at some point they had to make the decision as to whether they were going to have a string of Mars missions OR a Mars program. He went on to explain that a program looks to the future and each mission builds on the successes (and failures) of previous missions. It sounds minor but it had huge implications for NASA.

"I'm sure you see where I'm going with this. I can't tell you how much money to go into the hole on something like this. I can tell you, however, that you need to ask yourself a question about whether you're trying to launch individual missions or create a program. I personally think it's a dream with far bigger implications than even you realize, but that's just what I think."

I'm thankful to have a friend like this. I didn't quit the project, and it did, in fact, become a great success. Now I offer the same encouragement to you. Your dream is magnificent. And you will certainly want to quit. But don't do it. It will be worth it.

Why Dreamers Quit

My job as a Dream Year coach is to offer countermeasures to help every person withstand the attacks on their dream. It takes tremendous emotional fortitude to bring a dream to life. Like Frodo carrying the One Ring of Power in *The Lord of the Rings* to Mount Doom, you invite dark forces into your life that must be identified and defeated. Let's take a look at the top reasons why dreamers quit and what you can do to overcome them:

1. Hard Work

Just because it's your dream doesn't mean the work is any easier. In fact, that's why it's so difficult. You don't crave easy things. You yearn for things that lie outside your grasp. You have to work for them, fight for them, and strain to achieve them. When something appears to be easy for other people, it doesn't mean that it actually is. John Grisham, the most successful crime novelist of all time, once confessed, "Writing's still the most difficult job I've ever had. But it's worth it." If writing is still difficult for John Grisham, then why would your dream be any easier?

You can't make the work easier. You can only make yourself capable of working harder. And you *can* work harder. Just as I learned I hadn't been training hard enough for the high school basketball team, you are capable of accomplishing so much more than you realize. That's the beauty of your dream—it brings out the best version of you. You may have to get up earlier, stop watching as much TV, start working through lunch, and cross off more items on your to-do list each day. But you can work harder for a season.

2. Comfortable Alternatives

The moment you pursue your dream, the work gets harder; the pressure gets more intense; and the temptation to do something easier becomes stronger than ever. Suddenly, all of the comfortable alternatives call out to you. A good-paying job emerges. Your former boss says he'd like to hire you back with a raise. You experience financial hardship during the holiday season. Your car breaks down. That new piece of technology you've always wanted becomes available. And you find yourself longing for the comforts of your old cubicle with regular paychecks.

But don't do it. Remind yourself why you started dreaming in the first place. Remember the pain points, the problems, and the frustrations that propelled you out of that comfortable existence into the uncharted waters of possibility. If you're not careful, the comfortable alternatives in this life will lure you away from significance. Do whatever it takes to remind yourself that you don't want to go back. It may be easier there, but the frustration of that insignificant life will visit you once again. And next time, you won't be able to do a darn thing about it.

3. Setbacks

The founder of Starbucks, Howard Schultz, wrote in his book *Onward* that starting a new endeavor "will crush your heart like nothing else. It will deliver the most disappointing setbacks, but also the most extraordinary moments in life." In other words, if you're a dreamer, setbacks are the new normal. Your best customer will call to say she's going with someone else. The start-up funds you're counting on will fall through. A manufacturing delay with the product will sabotage your cash flow. And plans for the new location will collapse. You'll think the world is coming to an end.

If you're not prepared to handle these setbacks, each one will deliver a dream-crushing blow. You have to learn to absorb them, survive them, and keep moving forward. Here's what I've learned: Whenever a door closes, don't wallow in your misery or wait around. Go after the better thing. Don't downshift or get insecure. Don't settle for less or halt your progress. Know that something better was meant for you and go after it. Assume that Plan B was actually Plan A, undertaken in the wrong order. This mind-set has emboldened me in the face of every setback and failure, and it has always turned out for something better.

4. Indecision

One of the reasons writing a book is so difficult compared with other endeavors such as blogging or writing magazine articles is that a book seems so permanent. Every word carries greater weight when you know it's going to sit on a library shelf. Sensing the importance of their work, many authors can't decide which words to put down. Each one feels inadequate, so the manuscript sits unfinished inside a desk drawer.

I've seen the same thing happen to new charities, businesses, faith-based organizations, and community endeavors. The project drifts into an endless cycle of indecision. Maybe nobody quits, but nothing ever happens either. The dreamer keeps waiting for the right circumstances to come about, but they never do. The idea sits dormant for years until no one asks about it anymore.

Not deciding is the coward's way of quitting. If you're going to quit, don't let it come from inactivity. Quit only after you've failed gloriously. Don't walk away from unfinished work. Die trying. Doing the *wrong* thing is better than doing *no* thing because at least you learn something.

You can make the money back. You can get back on your feet. And you can try again. But you can never recover from what you didn't try at all.

5. Self-doubt

No matter how qualified, how capable, or how talented some people are, they just can't shake the notion that they're not good enough. Maybe the dream didn't happen fast enough. Maybe they couldn't be satisfied with their own work. Or maybe they were criticized one time too many. Whatever the reason, it wasn't credible, but it triggered something deep inside of them that caused them to walk away. They doubted themselves. And sadly, the defeat was entirely in their own minds.

Some people *should* doubt themselves. Seth Godin once said that "the person who is a really bad painter—not an edgy kind of painter, not a new kind of painter, just a bad painter—is bad at it because they can't see. They can't see the arc of a hundred paintings in a row and their painting. It's in a totally different league and they don't get it." He acknowledged that these people *should* quit.

"But if you can see that there is an arc," he added, "and your work belongs in that arc, you're going to make a different decision."

The arc to which Seth refers is the body of exceptional work that you are attempting to join with your own contribution. At first attempt, your work isn't going to stand up. If you doubt this, just search Katy Perry's, Lady Gaga's, or Justin Bieber's earliest recordings on YouTube. But if you have the potential to be good, the only thing that can derail you is your own self-doubt. Listen to what radio host Ira Glass had to say about getting better:

"Nobody tells this to people who are beginners. I wish someone told me. All of us who do creative work—we get into it because we have good taste. But there is this gap. For the first couple years you make stuff, it's just not that good. It's trying to be good, it has potential, but it's not. But your taste, the thing that got you into the game, is still killer. And your taste is why your work disappoints you. A lot of people never get past this phase. They quit. Most people I know who do interesting, creative work went through years of this. We know our work doesn't have this special thing that we want it to have. We all go through this. And if you are just starting out or you are still in this phase, you've got to know it's normal. And the most important thing you can do is to do a lot of work. Put yourself on a deadline so that every week you will finish one story. It is only by going through a volume of work that you will close that gap, and your work will be as good as your ambitions."

6. No Passion

Some people discover in the pursuit of their dream that they don't have the passion to sustain it. On November 6, 2012, the Grammy Award–winning band the Civil Wars posted this notice on their Facebook page:

We sincerely apologize for the canceling of all of our tour dates. It is something we deeply regret. However, due to internal discord and irreconcilable differences of ambition we are unable to continue as a touring entity at this time. We thank each and ev-

ery one of you for your amazing love & support. Our sincere
hope is to have new music for you in 2013.

—JOY WILLIAMS & JOHN PAUL WHITE

After roaring to the top of the music charts in 2011 with the release *Barton Hollow* and winning two Grammy Awards for the
Best Country Duo Performance and the Best Folk Album of 2012,
one of the band members lost the passion for touring.

Losing your passion is a sign of dream misalignment. It wasn't
something you really wanted after all. Maybe it was necessary for
your own personal development or the process of elimination.
Maybe it was meant to prepare you for something else. But it was an
artificial dream. When this happens, take stock of what you didn't
like about it and what you prefer instead. All of us have to make
course corrections along the way to arrive at our true dreams.

7. No Money

Without money, you worry about cash flow, paying the bills, and
getting things done with excellence. It adds stress to your life and
forces you to ask others for help. No one likes being a beggar. But it
doesn't mean you have to quit. Not having money doesn't make
your dream impossible, just inconvenient. There is always a way,
and as a dreamer, it is your necessary rite of passage to find it.

First, determine exactly how much money you need. Calculate all
of the costs in one grand total. Second, brainstorm all of the ways
you can acquire the funds. Could you work a second job? Will people donate money? Will they pay for your offering before it's created? Can you find investors? Do sponsorships apply? Is there a
partner who would share in the costs? Can you start a mobile version? Third, divide your grand total into smaller, more obtainable
increments of revenue. Asking for $100 from one hundred people is
much easier than asking for $10,000 from one person.

8. Unwillingness to Change

Your first try is not your only try. You don't have just one opportunity to launch an idea, after which you must scrap the entire dream if it doesn't work. You experiment your way into success. You make tweaks and adjustments until you find the formula that works best. There are no sacred tactics when it comes to your dream. But you need the humility to say goodbye to preferred approaches that clearly aren't working.

In 2010, Jason Goldberg and Bradford Shane Shellhammer realized their gay social networking site Fabulis.com wasn't working. It had grown to 130,000 members and got stuck. But rather than quitting everything, they shifted the business to a flash-sale Web site where members could get surprise deals on fashionable products for a limited time. They renamed the site Fab.com and grew it to 10 million members as of December 2012. They reached 1 million users faster than Twitter, Groupon, and Facebook. How many of us would have quit after the first attempt? Or how many of us would have been content with the initial 130,000 members?

Good comes at the expense of great.

9. An Employee Mind-set

There will be days when you long for the consistent paychecks, vacation time, and holiday office parties that come from conventional employment. There are creature comforts of having a regular job. It's a mind-set that allows you to relax, not worry about so many things, and just do what they hired you to do. But as long as you have more days when you celebrate the rewards of your dream than the times you long for comfort, you'll have the strength to carry on.

The challenge of your dream is to *not* think like an employee. Your dream needs a CEO. If you show up for work waiting for instructions and wondering what opportunities are going to come to you, you'll never make it. Just as every runner needs an internal "coach" to tell her to go out and run five miles, you need an internal "boss" to set the goals of your dream and compel the "workforce" to achieve them. If you show up every day as only the "workforce" with no boss in sight, pretty soon you'll be spending all your time playing Ping-Pong in the break room, and the whole business will go under.

10. Criticism

There's no avoiding it. You're going to be criticized for your dream. People have a penchant for pulling others down to their level. No one likes an outlier. They'll tell you it won't work. They won't understand why you're doing it. Your friends will tease you. Your relatives will encourage you to be more sensible. Strangers will ask questions that make you reconsider everything. And if you don't have the resolve to ignore it, you'll quit the very thing you were born to do.

You can't avoid critics. That's not a choice you have. But what you can choose is whether you'll listen to them. I'm convinced that the more criticism you face, the more impact your dream will have. Mahatma Gandhi once said: "First they ignore you, then they laugh at you, then they fight you, then you win."

John Bogle revolutionized the investment industry in 1974 by starting a company that focused on mutual funds, which weren't exactly lauded by Wall Street at the time. His company, the Vanguard Group, is now the largest investment fund group in the country, with thirteen thousand employees and $1.9 trillion in managed funds. At eighty-three years old, John admits that he had to sequester himself from critics, opinion surveys, and focus groups. Otherwise, he never would have taken the risks to start the company.

When Things Don't Go the Way You Saw Them Going

If you're a person with a plan, someone who saw it going a certain way, it doesn't matter if a change of plan is actually better for you. When change comes, it always feels like a crisis. Sometimes bad things happen. But most of the time, they're good things we paint as bad because they were unexpected. A new season in your life always feels like things are falling apart at first. But they're not. They're making way.

Think about it. If there's a better plan in store for you, something has to dislodge you from your established plan in order to make way for the better one. Your plan *has* to fail. The question is, will you turn off the warning sirens, stop fretting, call off the crisis, come out of depression, and let the better thing happen?

When our ideas begin to sink, many of us watch them go down, shrug our shoulders, and say, "Well, I guess that idea wasn't meant to be."

But you're supposed to fight for them. Dreams are supposed to be hard work. They're not supposed to happen on their own. They need you to save them.

Never Give Up

Some ideas appear to succeed overnight. But don't be fooled. By now, you know that dreams come to life by one corrective turn after another. Just as rock bands win Grammy Awards for "best new artist" after years of recording and touring, successful start-ups are celebrated as new discoveries after years of hard work, trial and error, and perseverance. There are no overnight successes. There are no epiphanies. And there is no luck.

Never look back unless you are planning to go that way.

—HENRY DAVID THOREAU

Coleman Cox said, "I am a great believer in luck, and I find the harder I work, the more I have of it."

If your dream doesn't take off right away, you're in good company. Most successful ideas fail to capture an audience the first year. Sometimes you need more experience before you can bring the idea to life. When Christopher Nolan first pitched a movie about dream stealers to Warner Bros. in 2001, he didn't get the reaction he wanted. He hadn't earned the credibility and trust to make such a complex and expensive film. So he kept revising the screenplay while gaining experience with other films. He went on to write and direct *Batman Begins*, *The Prestige*, *The Dark Knight*, and *Memento*. Nine years later, he was ready to go back to his first idea, which the studios gladly embraced. That movie was *Inception*, which won four Academy Awards and earned more than $825 million at the box office, making it one of the highest-grossing films of all time.

Sometimes it takes awhile for people to embrace your idea. Novelist Ken Follett spent three exhausting years writing a 400,000-word story about the construction of a cathedral called *The Pillars of the Earth*. The publisher was nervous about investing in such an obscure and lengthy project. And even Ken's friends questioned whether he should stray from his usual spy novels.

When the book was released in 1989, reviews were mixed, and it failed to find an audience right away. But over the next decade, the book built a steady readership. By 2003, it was ranked thirty-third in a survey by the BBC to discover England's all-time favorite books. In 2007, Oprah selected it for her book club, and the paperback version spent thirty weeks on the *New York Times* bestseller list. *The Pillars of the Earth* has been published in thirty languages and has sold more than 15 million copies. It continues to sell more than 100,000 copies a year.

ABRAHAM LINCOLN'S CAREER OF NOT QUITTING

1816—His family was forced out of their home. He had to work to support them.

1818—His mother died.

1831—Failed in business.

1832—Ran for state legislature and lost.

1832—He also lost his job. Wanted to go to law school but couldn't get in.

1833—He borrowed some money from a friend to start a business but went bankrupt. He spent the next seventeen years of his life paying off this debt.

1834—He ran for state legislature again and won.

1835—He was engaged to be married, but his fiancée died, leaving him heartbroken.

1836—He had a nervous breakdown and was in bed for six months.

1838—He tried to become speaker of the state legislature but was defeated.

1840—He sought to become an elector but was defeated.

1843—He ran for U.S. Congress and lost.

1846—He ran for U.S. Congress again and won.

1848—He ran for reelection to Congress and lost.

1849—He sought the job of land officer in his home state and was rejected.

1854—He ran for U.S. Senate and lost.

1856—He sought the vice presidential nomination and got fewer than one hundred votes.

1858—He ran for U.S. Senate again and lost.

1860—He ran for president and won.

The Willingness to Walk Away

Sometimes walking away from a dream is not failure, but the ultimate expression of success. After all, you are more than your dream. It was meant to be your legacy but not define you. At some moment, when the end of your life comes, you'll have no choice but to let it go. Until then, it's perfectly acceptable to let it go on your own volition. A dream is meant to be your gift to the world. If you did it right, other people will own it through their loyalty and passion for the brand.

In October 2012, George Lucas sold his *Stars Wars* franchise to Disney for $4.05 billion. The announcement worried countless fans who feared that Disney would ruin the story. But George knew he was holding back his own dream. *Star Wars* had become much larger than Lucasfilm could handle on its own. Disney offered the chance to extend the brand with additional episodes, interactive media, theme parks, live entertainment, and products.

George said, "It is now time for me to pass *Star Wars* on to a new generation of filmmakers. I've always believed that *Star Wars* could live beyond me, and I thought it was important to set up the transition during my lifetime."

There's nothing worse than a poorly stewarded dream, where the creator hangs on for too long. Who can forget the awkward retirement of basketball superstar Michael Jordan, who quit in 1993; then played minor league baseball in Birmingham, Alabama; came back to play basketball in 1994; retired again in 1999; and then played again for the Washington Wizards in 2001 before being fired by the organization at the end of the season?

It was an inglorious thing to watch.

When comedian Jerry Seinfeld ended his successful TV show *Seinfeld*, he was on top of the network ratings. But he didn't want to hobble off the lineup after viewers stopped watching. He said, "I wanted to end the show on the same kind of peak we've been doing it on for years. I wanted the end to be from a point of strength. I wanted the end to be graceful."

Part of the success of your dream is what you do with it when it's time to walk away. It could be that you don't have the ability to take it to another level. You need the help of other leaders. But another reason to walk away is to take full advantage of the value of your organization while you're still alive. After starting Behance in 2006, Scott Belsky grew the number of members on his portfolio site to 1 million people before selling the company to Adobe for $150 million in December 2012. Scott could have continued to grow the company on his own, but he decided to get an immediate return on his hard work and investment.

Quitting is not just an exit. It's the beginning of a new dream, but this time with more resources, more knowledge, and more experience. Sometimes walking away is the best move you can make.

Call to Action

The worst time to think about quitting is when you're in the throes of pursuing your dream. If you haven't thought about it before, you'll be tempted to give up at every hint of hardship along the way. Give your will a chance to stand up to your whim. Make a list of the conditions that must be in place before you'll quit—the criteria for quitting, if you will. What would make you walk away? Write them down now.

I'm certain you can withstand more difficulty than you think. Play out the worst-case scenario in your head. What's the worst that could happen?

Just because it's your dream doesn't mean it's going to be easy. In fact, this will be harder than anything else you've ever done. But the reward is so much bigger. It's worth the fight. So don't quit. Never give up. Refuse to walk away. Or you'll end up right back where you started, plagued by a frustration you never resolved. And the world will miss out on a great dream that only you can turn into reality.

QUESTIONS:

1. What temptations to quit are you currently facing? Are the circumstances more than you can bear? Is it one of the conditions you specified?
2. Imagine your dream fully realized. Is it worth the hardship you're experiencing? Can you adapt and endure for a season?
3. Don't struggle in isolation. What new habits or relationships do you need to form to ensure that you'll persevere? Don't be afraid to ask for help.

Go confidently in the direction of your dreams.
Live the life you have imagined.

—HENRY DAVID THOREAU

ACKNOWLEDGMENTS

The author wishes to thank his wife, Ainsley, and his children for giving him the time and inspiration to write this book. He would also like to thank Curtis Yates for sharing his vision of what the book could be and Maria Gagliano for believing in the book and shaping the content. Finally, he would like to thank the participants of Dream Year's coaching program and weekend retreats for the examples and insights and you, the reader, for helping to bring the dream of this book to life.

NOTES

CHAPTER 1

5 **"When Fred Astaire and Michael Jackson"**: Joan Acocella, "Walking on the Moon," *The New Yorker*, July 27, 2009, www.newyorker.com/arts/critics/dancing/2009/07/27/090727crda_dancing_accella.

6 **"When Howard was a small child"**: Richard McGill Murphy, "Businessperson of the Year," *Fortune*, Dec. 12, 2011, 112.

6 **"a broken hip and ankle"**: Kathryn Dill, "By Their Bootstraps: Billionaires Who Started from Scratch," *Forbes*, Sept. 18, 2013, www.forbes.com/sites/kathryndill/2013/09/18/by-their-bootstraps-billionaires-who-started-from-scratch.

7 **"we must *make* our own jobs"**: Jocelyn K. Glei, "Why Entrepreneurial Thinking Is for Everyone Now," the99percent.com, http://99u.com/articles/7161/why-entrepreneurial-thinking-is-for-everyone-now.

7 **"our generation of entrepreneurs"**: Thomas Fisher, "The Next Economy and the 'Next Politics,'" *The Huffington Post*, Feb. 1, 2012, www.huffingtonpost.com/thomas-fisher/the-next-economy-and-the-_b_1243168.html.

7 **"66 percent of Americans hate their jobs"**: Susan Steinbrecher, "Why Half of America Hates Their Jobs," http://www.cnbc.com/id/47875050.

7 **"UPS found that 48 percent of Americans"**: David Meilach, "Who Wants to Be an Entrepreneur? 48% of Americans, That's Who," *Business News Daily*, accessed June 6, 2012, /www.businessnewsdaily.com/4648-small-business-challenges.html.

8 **"there are only 1.2 billion full-time, formal jobs"**: Ben Casnocha, "Notes from Books About Jobs and Work," http://casnocha.com/2012/02/notes-from-books-about-jobs-and-work.html?utm_source=feedburner&utm_medium=feed&utm_campaign=Feed:+bencasnocha+%28Ben+Casnocha:+The+Blog%29.

8 **"12.7 million people remain unemployed"**: www.bls.gov/opub/
   ted/2012/ted_20120710.htm.

8 **"started the State Bicycle Co."** "Bicycle Startup Wins Uphill
   Race," www.amazon.com/gp/feature.html?ie=UTF8&docId=1000
   807561.

8 **"In just four years, they opened three stores"**: Ellen Lee, "Millennial
   Entrepreneurs Bypass the Unemployment Line," *USA Today*, Nov.
   30, 2011, accessed June 16, 2012, http://usatoday30.usatoday.com/
   money/smallbusiness/story/2011-12-03/cnbc-millennial-
   entrepreneurs/51513386/1.

8 **"designing a house for the entrepreneurial age"**: "LiveWork: The
   Future of Living Where You Work and Working Where You Live,"
   Co.Exist, www.fastcoexist.com/1679317/livework-the-future-of-living
   -where-you-work-and-working-where-you-live.

8 **"At the 2009 Kentucky Derby"**: "Mine That Bird," http://www
   .youtube.com/watch?v=Hv8x9x5A49s.

9 **"I rode him like a good horse"**: http://sports.espn.go.com/sports/
   horse/triplecrown09/news/story?id=4128767.

11 **"producing comedies such as *It's Always Sunny in Philadelphia*"**:
   "FX Networks," *Fast Company*, Mar. 2011, 117.

11 **"Edward Burns has been making movies"**: http://en.wikipedia.org/
   wiki/Edward_Burns.

13 **"In an interview with ESPN, Malcolm Gladwell"**: Jeff Merron,
   "Interview: Malcolm Gladwell," ESPN, http://sports.espn.go.com/
   espn/page2/story?page=merron/050203.

15 **"*The New York Times* printed the obituary"**: Margalit Fox, "John
   Fairfax, Who Rowed Across Oceans, Dies at 74," *The New York
   Times*, www.nytimes.com/2012/02/19/us/john-fairfax-who-rowed
   -across-oceans-dies-at-74.html?_r=4&.

CHAPTER 2

20 **"Career expert Penelope Trunk once wrote"**: Penelope Trunk,
   "Why You Already Know What You Should Be Doing Next,"
   May 12, 2008, http://blog.penelopetrunk.com/2008/05/12/why-you
   -already-know-what-you-should-be-doing-next/.

21 **"The movie director Guillermo del Toro"**: Daniel Zalewski, "Show
   the Monster," *The New Yorker*, Feb. 7, 2011, 41.

24 **"In an interview with James Lipton:** *Inside the Actors Studio*,

www.bravotv.com/inside-the-actors-studio/season-19/videos/
classic-episode-steven-spielberg.

24 **"this record is my way of getting the albums"**: John McPhee, "The
Musical Life," *The New Yorker*, Feb. 7, 2011, 24.

25 **"a magazine called *Student*"**: http://en.wikipedia.org/wiki/Richard
_Branson.

25 **"But I soon found I had to become an entrepreneur"**: Brad Dunn,
*When They Were 22: 100 Famous People at the Turning Point of
Their Lives* (Andrews McMeel Publishing, 2006), 16.

26 **"Tomorrow would be better"**: Seth Godin, "Was Google Right to Be
So Sure of Themselves?," Mar. 21, 2007, http://sethgodin.typepad
.com/the_dip/2007/03/was_google_righ.html.

27 **" 'But he did. . . . That's why it's here' "**: http://disneyparks.disney.
go.com/blog/2010/05/a-moment-with-art/.

28 **"As a teenager . . . by quitting a job at McDonald's"**: Nicholas
Carlson, "Jeff Bezos: Here's Why He Won," *Business Insider*, May
16, 2011, accessed June 16, 2012, www.businessinsider.com/jeff
-bezos-visionary-2011-4.

30 **"If content is king, distribution is King Kong"**: Allison Dollar, "Internet Convergence Dominates MobileMonday Global Summit,"
accessed June 12, 2012, http://mobilemonday.com.ua/news/press/
internet-convergence.html.

31 **"he was named Producer of the Year"**: http://en.wikipedia.org/
wiki/Ed_Cash.

32 **"But I think I write about science more clearly"**: Jeff Merron, "Interview: Malcolm Gladwell," ESPN, http://sports.espn.go.com/
espn/page2/story?page=merron/050203.

35 **"He refused to answer on the grounds"**: Robbie Coltrane, http://
www.nbcnews.com/id/4558561#.UtlcAvYo6Rs.

36 **"Yet most of us only look at how that same typewriter"**: http://
en.wikipedia.org/wiki/Cormac_McCarthy.

38 **"Vitamins are nice; they're healthy"**: Dan Heath and Chip Heath,
"Turning Vitamins into Aspirin: Consumers and the 'Felt Need,' "
Fast Company, Nov. 2, 2010, www.fastcompany.com/1693729/
turning-vitamins-aspirin-consumers-and-felt-need.

38 **"When Chuck Templeton created"**: Soren Kaplan, "How to Turn a
Nasty Surprise into the Next Disruptive Idea," Fastcodesign.com,
June 11, 2012, www.fastcodesign.com/1670007/how-to-turn-a
-nasty-surprise-into-the-next-disruptive-idea.

38 **"OpenTable now serves"**: http://en.wikipedia.org/wiki/OpenTable.

39 **"Author Steven Pressfield describes the phenomenon"**: Steven Pressfield, *Turning Pro: Tap Your Inner Power and Create Your Life's Work* (Black Irish Entertainment LLC, 2012), 13.

CHAPTER 3

43 **"The business spread from Boston to Washington, D.C."**: Dinah Eng, "Zipcar Founder's Second Act," *Fortune*, Dec. 3, 2012, 33.

43 **"In March 2013, Avis purchased Zipcar"**: Ryan Bradley, "Their Revolution," *Fortune*, Oct. 28, 2013, 34.

44 **"Fabien created Future Cinema"**: http://en.wikipedia.org/wiki/Future _Cinema.

45 **"People want to experience culture"**: Felicity White, "The Secret of Cinema," StoryChicago.com, Feb. 4, 2013, http://storychicago .com/updates/secret-cinema.

45 **"they had collected props such as satin Pink Ladies"**: "In Pictures: Behind the Scenes at Future Cinema's 'Grease' Summer Love-in," http://now-here-this.timeout.com/2012/09/05/in-pictures-behind -the-scenes-at-future-cinemas-grease-summer-love-in/.

45 **"They had more ticket sales"**: Leo Barraclough, "Secret Cinema Heads for Gotham," *Variety*, Oct. 20, 2012, http://variety.com/ 2012/film/news/secret-cinema-heads-for-gotham-1118061032/.

45 **"Even more, he recently launched Secret Restaurant"**: Natasha Stokes, "The Rise of 'Secret Tourism' Covert Cinema Evenings, Surprise Dinners and Now Clandestine Hotels—Why Some People Are Happy to Pay Before They Know What They're Going to Get," *CNN Travel*, Nov. 19, 2012, http://travel.cnn.com/fly-night-rise -secret-night-out-739916?cid=sf_twitter.

46 **"They launched Airbnb in 2008"**: http://en.wikipedia.org/wiki/ Airbnb.

46 **"by February 2012, reported more than 5 million nights"**: Chris Taylor, "The Unstoppable Rise of Airbnb," *Mashable*, Jan. 26, 2012, http://mashable.com/2012/01/26/airbnb-infographic/.

46 **"People simply log on to their Skype accounts"**: Gabrielle Bell, Dec. 7, 2012, http://gabriellebell.com/2012/12/07/some-portraits/.

46 **"Eleven seamstresses produce six thousand pairs a year"**: Lauren Murrow, "The Factory's in the Back," *New York Magazine*, May 8, 2011, http://nymag.com/shopping/openings/3x1-scott-morrison -2011-5/.

46 **"Every Book a Surprise"**: Biblio-Mat, "Book Vending Machine Dispenses Suspense," NPR Books, Nov. 18, 2012, www.npr.org/2012/11/18/165219956/book-vending-machine-dispenses-suspense.

46 **"Manpacks, which ships undergarments"**: Shivani Vora, "Underwear by Subscription: Will It Be a Fit for Busy Men?" *Inc.*, Oct. 2010.

47 **"More than twenty-four thousand people have signed up"**: Claire Evans, "The Luck of the Listserve," *The New Inquiry*, May 14, 2013, http://thenewinquiry.com/essays/the-luck-of-the-listserve/.

47 **"He's defying the elite art world"**: Alessandro di Fiore, "At the High End, Reaching a Mass Market," *Harvard Business Review*, Nov. 9, 2012, http://blogs.hbr.org/2012/11/at-the-high-end-reaching-a-mass-market/.

47 **"The company processes more than \$350 million"**: Alyson Shontell, "This 28-Year-Old's Startup Is Moving \$350 Million and Wants to Completely Kill Credit Cards," *Business Insider*, Nov. 11, 2011, www.businessinsider.com/this-28-year-old-is-making-sure-credit-cards-wont-exist-in-the-next-few-years-2011-11#ixzz2qlXiz8KG.

49 **"Research shows that digital downloads"**: Aaron Baar, "Digital Movies Gaining in Popularity," *MediaPost*, Oct. 22, 2012, www.mediapost.com/publications/article/185652/digital-movies-gaining-in-popularity.html?e3540b4c=&f9009fb5=t.

50 **"actors dressed in period costumes"**: Michael Schulman, "Poster Girls," *The New Yorker*, July 27, 2009, www.newyorker.com/talk/2009/07/27/090727ta_talk_schulman.

50 **"*TV Guide* placed *Mad Men* sixth"**: http://en.wikipedia.org/wiki/Mad_Men.

51 **"legend about a university president who refused"**: Derek Sivers, "Let Pedestrians Define the Walkways," Nov. 23, 2011, http://sivers.org/walkways.

51 **"Drew Houston asked himself why people"**: Greg McAdoo, "How to Choose Your Startup Idea," *TechCrunch*, Oct. 19, 2012, http://techcrunch.com/2012/10/19/how-to-choose-your-startup-idea/.

51 **"The result was Dropbox, which now has"**: Josh Constine, "Dropbox Now Has 175 Million Users, Up from 100M in November 2012," *TechCrunch*, July 9, 2013, http://techcrunch.com/2013/07/09/dropbox-dbx-conference/.

54 **"Andrew Mason from Chicago started a Web site"**: http://en.wikipedia.org/wiki/Groupon.

54 "You know the Web site as Groupon": Adam K. Raymond, "The Tipping Point," United.com, Nov. 2010, 54–57.

55 "He likes it because he knows 'it's doing what it's supposed to do'": Ariel Levy, "Brand-New Bag," *The New Yorker*, Apr. 25, 2011, www.newyorker.com/reporting/2011/04/25/110425fa_fact _levy.

55 "He knows the last page of the book": Dennis Moore, "John Grisham Marks 20th Anniversary of 'A Time to Kill,'" *USA Today*, June 22, 2009, http://usatoday30.usatoday.com/life/books/news/2009-06-21-john-grisham-a-time-to-kill_N.htm.

56 "He has a passion for his craft": Seth Godin, *Linchpin: Are You Indispensable?* (Portfolio, 2011).

CHAPTER 4

59 "Business author Barbara Stanny describes": Jocelyn K. Glei, "Are You a Serial Under-Earner?," 99u.com, http://99u.com/tips/6974/Are-You-A-Serial-Under-Earner.

61 "President Daniel Lamarre described three criteria": Emily Wexler, "C2-MTL: The Business of Storytelling, and How to Make a Circus," *Media in Canada*, May 25, 2012, http://mediaincanada.com/2012/05/25/c2-mtl-the-business-of-storytelling-and-how-to-make-a-circus/#ixzz2qlk3paBZ.

64 "Chef Frances Kroner in Cincinnati": www.feastcincinnati.com.

65 "only 10 percent of the population goes to movie theaters": Edward Jay Epstein, *The Hollywood Economist* (Melville House, 2010).

68 "Competitor Group has figured out how to create": Matt McCue, "Competitor Group Inc. on Racing to Gain Digital Dollars," *Fast Company*, Sept. 12, 2012, www.fastcompany.com/3000881/competitor-group-inc-racing-gain-digital-dollars.

68 "John Saddington in Atlanta has worked his way": John Saddington, Nov. 20, 2010, www.tentblogger.com/full-time-blogger.

70 "he sold 110,000 subscriptions for a total of $550,000": Stephen Shankland, "Wake Up, Media Moguls: Louis C.K. No-DRM Video Makes $200K," *CNET*, Dec. 14, 2011, http://news.cnet.com/8301-30685_3-57342775-264/wake-up-media-moguls-louis-c.k-no-drm-video-makes-$200k/.

70 "This is exactly what happened in 2009": http://en.wikipedia.org/wiki/Uber_%28company%29.

71 **"a leaked financial statement showed that Uber"**: Caroline Moss, "Leaked Financials Show Uber Brings In About $20 Million per Week," *Business Insider*, Dec. 4, 2013, www.businessinsider.com/ leaked-uber-financials-2013-12.

71 **"He describes eight revenue models"**: Ryan Baum, "Want to Upend an Entire Industry? Change Its Revenue Stream," *Co.Design*, Oct. 18, 2011, www.fastcodesign.com/1665228/want-to-upend-an-entire -industry-change-its-revenue-stream.

71 **"Zumba's Portfolio of Revenue"**: Leigh Buchanan, "Zumba Fitness: Company of the Year," *Inc.*, Dec. 4, 2012, http://www.inc. com/magazine/201212/leigh-buchanan/zumba-fitness-company -of-the-year-2012.html.

73 **"she crafted a shabby chic exhibit"**: Brad Dunn, *When They Were 22: 100 Famous People at the Turning Point of Their Lives.* (Andrews McMeel Publishing, 2006).

74 **"Fast food restaurants do this all the time"**: Kate Rockwood, "From Taco Bell to IHOP, Fast-Food Goes Upscale or Scales Down for New Audiences," *Fast Company*, Sept. 12, 2012, www.fast-company.com/3000849/taco-bell-ihop-fast-food-goes-upscale-or -scales-down-new-audiences.

75 **"The same factory in Israel that makes Jordache"**: Matthew Boyle and Lauren Coleman-Lochner, "Whatever Happened to Jordache?" *Bloomberg Businessweek*, July 26, 2012, www.business week.com/articles/2012-07-26/whatever-happened-to-jordache.

75 **"Blake Butler bought a snow globe"**: Blake Butler, "Utah Snow Globe," SignificantObjects.com, Mar. 5, 2010, http://significant objects.com/2010/03/05/utah-snow-globe-blake-butler-story/.

75 **"After writing a fantastical and somewhat ridiculous story"**: Duke Greenhill, "How to Sell a $1 Snow Globe for $59: The Real ROI of Brand Storytelling," *Fast Company*, Nov. 8, 2012, www.fastcompany .com/3002804/how-sell-1-snow-globe-59-real-roi-brand-story telling.

75 **"Business consultant Neil Baron wrote about"**: Neil Baron, "How to Charge Higher Prices and Thrive," *Fast Company*, Dec. 19, 2011, www.fastcompany.com/1801522/how-charge-higher-prices -and-thrive.

76 **"We're in a service economy now"**: Jason Fried and David Heinemeier Hansson, *Rework* (Crown Business, 2010), 50.

CHAPTER 5

83 "The app grew to 54.7 million active users a month": Todd Wasserman, "Autodesk Buys Socialcam for $60 Million," *Mashable*, July 17, 2012, http://mashable.com/2012/07/17/autodesk-buys-social cam/.

84 "If we hadn't started then, what would we have later?": Justin Kan, "Why Starting Justin.tv Was a Really Bad Idea, But I'm Glad We Did It Anyway," *TechCrunch*, Feb. 12, 2011, http://techcrunch.com /2011/02/12/starting-justin-tv/.

84 "They created fifty-one games and nearly went bankrupt": Josh Linkner, "The Dirty Little Secret of Overnight Successes," *Fast Company*, Apr. 3, 2012, www.fastcompany.com/1826976/dirty -little-secret-overnight-successes.

84 "has been downloaded more than two billion times": Frans Johansson, "When Success Is Born Out of Serendipity," *Harvard Business Review*, Oct. 19, 2012, http://blogs.hbr.org/2012/10/when-success -is-born-out-of-serendipity/.

85 "Michael Gerber describes how he accidentally stumbled": Michael E. Gerber, *The E-Myth Revisited: Why Most Small Businesses Don't Work and What to Do About It* (HarperCollins, 1995).

85 "Here's what their Imagineers wrote": Theodore Kinni, *Be Our Guest* (Disney Editions, 2011).

88 "When Will Smith appeared on *The Tavis Smiley Show*": Tavis Smiley, Dec. 13, 2007, http://www.youtube.com/watch?v=doqS35FfcUE &feature=youtu.be.

88 "In his must-read book *The War of Art*": Steven Pressfield, *The War of Art: Break Through the Blocks and Win Your Inner Creative Battles* (Black Irish Entertainment, 2012).

93 "Anne Lamott once wrote: 'I sometimes teach classes on writing'": Anne Lamott, "Time Lost and Found," *Sunset*, Apr. 2010, www .sunset.com//travel/anne-lamott-how-to-find-time-0041800006 7331/.

93 "In the average televised broadcast of an NFL football game": "During an NFL Game, the Ball Is in Play Less Than 11 Minutes," *Spirit Magazine*, Jan. 2011, 36.

101 "These 'great groups' have a few characteristics": Warren Bennis and Patricia Ward Biederman, *Organizing Genius: The Secrets of Creative Collaboration* (Basic Books, 1998), 4–10.

101 "Michelangelo wasn't a solitary artist": Ibid., 5.

CHAPTER 6

105   **"In the case of Apple stores, the average employee"**: Henry Blodget, "17 Facts About the Apple Store Profit Machine," *Business Insider*, June 25, 2012, www.businessinsider.com/apple-store-facts-2012-6?op=1#ixzz2qmax558P.

106   **"And Bob took his kids to every one of these meetings"**: Bob Goff, "Finding Incredible Experiences in Ordinary Life," *Fast Company*, Aug. 13, 2012, www.fastcompany.com/3000393/finding-incredible-experiences-ordinary-life.

109   **"In his bestselling book *The 4-Hour Work Week* ..."**: Timothy Ferriss, *The 4-Hour Work Week: Escape the 9–5, Live Anywhere and Join the New Rich* (Harmony, 2009).

110   **"Babe Ruth held Major League Baseball's career *strikeout record*"**: Simon Sinek, "Are You Willing to Strike Out?," *AskMen*, www.askmen.com/money/career_300/372_are-you-willing-to-strike-out-simon-sinek.html.

114   **"Nike once aired a commercial featuring this confession"**: www.youtube.com/watch?v=45mMioJ5szc.

CHAPTER 7

121   **"If it feels off, or like it compromises who we are"**: Valentine Freeman, "Everything's Aces," StoryChicago.com, Feb. 28, 2013, http://storychicago.com/updates/everythings-aces.

121   **"There are more than forty whiskeys on the menu"**: John Rambow, "Creative Destinations: In Chicago, a Buzzy Restaurant Becomes an Artsy Hotel," *Co.design*, Jan. 11, 2011, www.fastcodesign.com/1663016/creative-destinations-in-chicago-a-buzzy-restaurant-becomes-an-artsy-hotel.

122   **"they make the experience more personal by posting signs"**: Michael Pavone, "How Whole Foods Became the Luxury Brand of Millennials," *Co.exist*, Feb. 23, 2012, www.fastcoexist.com/1679351/how-whole-foods-became-the-luxury-brand-of-millennials.

124   **"Paul Smailes ... chose an older man"**: E. J. Schultz, "How This Man Made Dos Equis a Most Interesting Marketing Story," *Creativity*, Mar. 5, 2012, http://creativity-online.com/news/the-story-behind-dos-equis-most-interesting-man-in-the-world/233112.

125   **"The brand consultancy Interbrand came up with"**: www.interbrand.com/en/our-work/MICROSOFT-BING.aspx.

128 "He promptly changed the name of his company": Matthew Panzarino, "Jack Dorsey Gives Us a Brief Look Back at Squirrel, the Square That Never Was," *TNW*, Sept. 11, 2012, http://thenextweb.com/insider/2012/09/11/jack-dorsey-gives-us-brief-look-back-squirrel-square-never/#!sy87L.

128 "The Stories Behind the Names": J. R. Raphael, "Why Are They Called That? The Silly Stories Behind Six Tech Brands," *TechHive*, Oct. 19, 2012, www.techhive.com/article/2012669/why-are-they-called-that-the-silly-stories-behind-six-tech-brands.html.

128 "The Stories Behind the Names": Alyson Shontell, "Zynga, Hulu and GoDaddy: Where 15 of the Strangest Company Names Came From," *Business Insider*, July 12, 2011, www.businessinsider.com/zynga-hulu-and-godaddy-where-15-of-the-strangest-startup-names-came-from-2011-7?op=1#ixzz2qmk7N5o5.

131 "David Butler . . . developed a book of standards": Linda Tischler, "Pop Artist: David Butler," *Fast Company*, Sept. 10, 2009, www.fastcompany.com/design/2009/featured-story-david-butler.

CHAPTER 8

138 "People don't have time to research all of the options": Seth Godin, *The Dip: A Little Book That Teaches You When to Quit (and When to Stick)* (Portfolio, 2007).

139 "the largest amount ever raised on Kickstarter until that date": Yancey Strickler, "Saving *Blue Like Jazz*," Kickstarter Blog, Oct. 25, 2010, www.kickstarter.com/blog/saving-blue-like-jazz.

140 "the WWE took notice and gave him more time on air": Jefferson Graham, "Ryder Harnesses Web to Boost His Career," *USA Today*, Jan. 29, 2012, www.usatoday.com/tech/columnist/talkingyourtech/story/2012-01-29/wwe-zack-ryder-youtube-internet-champion/52873304/1.

142 "At the 2011 Dartmouth College commencement": Conan O'Brien's Dartmouth Commencement Address, www.youtube.com/watch?v=KmDYXaaT9sA&feature=youtu.be.

143 "It wasn't until *Salon* had the courage to embrace its expertise": Kerry Lauerman, "Hit Record," *Salon*, Feb. 7, 2012, http://open.salon.com/blog/kerry_lauerman/2012/02/03/hit_record.

144 "she launched Spanx": http://en.wikipedia.org/wiki/Spanx.

144 "She said, 'I keep saying this to the team'": Alexandra Jacobs, "Smooth Moves," *The New Yorker*, Mar. 28, 2011, www.newyorker.com/reporting/2011/03/28/110328fa_fact_jacobs.

147 *"Wired,* cofounder Kevin Kelly"*: Seth Godin, "1000 True Fans," Sethgodin.typepad.com, Mar. 4, 2008, http://sethgodin.typepad.com/seths_blog/2008/03/1000-true-fans.html.

149 "Her advertising revenue alone brought in": Amanda Fortini, "O Pioneer Woman!" *The New Yorker,* May 9, 2011, www.newyorker.com/reporting/2011/05/09/110509fa_fact_fortini.

150 "In the 1990s, billionaire Phil Anschutz": http://en.wikipedia.org/wiki/Philip_Anschutz.

151 "Stephen King once tweeted": https://twitter.com/StephenKing/status/409068267362197504.

152 "TubeMogul estimates that in 2012": Amy O'Leary, "The Woman with 1 Billion Clicks, Jenna Marbles," *The New York Times,* Apr. 12, 2013, www.nytimes.com/2013/04/14/fashion/jenna-marbles.html?_r=2&pagewanted=all&.

152 "analysts put it at 10 million people": Owen Thomas, "Amazon Has an Estimated 10 Million Members for Its Suprisingly Profitable Prime Club," *Business Insider,* Mar. 11, 2013, www.businessinsider.com/amazon-prime-10-million-members-morningstar-2013-3.

153 "By the fourth month, there were 30 million views": Kym McNicholas, "Marquese Scott: An Overnight Sensation?" *Forbes,* Feb. 2, 2012, www.forbes.com/sites/kymmcnicholas/2012/02/02/marquese-scott-an-overnight-sensation/.

153 "by the printing of this book, there have been nearly 103 million views": Marquese Scott, www.youtube.com/watch?v=LXO-jKksQkM.

153 "Scott Harrison spent ten years promoting": Scott Harrison's story, www.charitywater.org/about/scotts_story.php, and http://en.wikipedia.org/wiki/Scott_Harrison_%28charity_founder%29.

154 "Amanda published her own e-book on Amazon": Ed Pilkington, "Amanda Hocking, the Writer Who Made Millions by Self-Publishing Online," *The Guardian,* Jan. 12, 2012, www.theguardian.com/books/2012/jan/12/amanda-hocking-self-publishing.

154 "she was offered a multimillion-dollar contract": Deirdre Donahue, "Paranormal Romance Writer Amanda Hocking Scored with E-books," *USA Today,* Jan. 3, 2012, http://usatoday30.usatoday.com/life/books/news/story/2012-01-03/amanda-hocking-self-published-author/52345642/1.

155 "the event was ranked by *Fast Company*": Jason Del Rey, "30 Under 30: Elliott Bisnow," *Inc.,* www.inc.com/30under30/2009/profile_summit_series.html.

156 "Web guru Chris Brogan wrote": Chris Brogan, "Chores," Nov. 21, 2010, www.chrisbrogan.com/chores/.

157 "One of the ways that political experts said Barack Obama beat Mitt Romney": Michael Kranish, "The Story Behind Mitt Romney's Loss in the Presidential Campaign to President Obama," *The Boston Globe*, Dec. 22, 2012, www.boston.com/news/politics/2012/president/2012/12/23/the-story-behind-mitt-romney-loss-the-presidential-campaign-president-obama/2QWkUB9pJgVIi1m AcIhQjL/story.html.

CHAPTER 9

162 "Rather than aiming for CEOs, he targeted diversity leaders": Frans Johansson, "When Success Is Born out of Serendipity," *Harvard Business Review*, Oct. 19, 2012, http://blogs.hbr.org/2012/10/when-success-is-born-out-of-serendipity/.

162 "the national college ministry Campus Crusade purchased 65,000 copies": David Dunlap, "Don Miller & *Blue Like Jazz*," *Bible & Life*, Jan. 1, 2008, www.bibleandlife.org/Newsletters/BL-2008/bibleandlife_2008_1.htm.

163 "It spent forty-three weeks on the *New York Times* bestseller list": John Blake, "Donald Miller's 'Blue Like Jazz' Film Set to Open," *CNN*, Mar. 9, 2012, http://religion.blogs.cnn.com/2012/03/09/donald-millers-blue-like-jazz-film-set-to-open/.

165 "He generated more than 209,000 page views": Dodd Caldwell, "How My Side Project Generated Sales and 66,000 Unique Visitors in 1 Month," *Dodd's Blog*, Mar. 31, 2012, http://blog.doddcaldwell.com/post/20238528691/how-my-side-project-generated-sales-and-66-000-unique.

167 "the jump was streamed live on YouTube for more than 8 million viewers": http://en.wikipedia.org/wiki/Red_Bull_Stratos.

167 "Since the beginning, it has been a brand philosophy": Teressa Iezzi, "Red Bull CEO Dietrich Mateschitz on Brand as Media Company," *Co.Create*, Feb. 17, 2012, www.fastcocreate.com/1679907/red-bull-ceo-dietrich-mateschitz-on-brand-as-media-company.

168 "more than forty thousand people converge at the corner of Surf and Stillwell avenues": www.nathansfamous.com/index.php/hot-dog-eating-contest.

168 "When rap artist Jay-Z's autobiography *Decoded*": Teressa Iezzi, "Cannes Jay-Z 'Decoded' Campaign Wins Integrated Grand Prix

and Titanium at Cannes," *Co.Create*, June 25, 2011, www.fastco
create.com/1679205/jay-z-decoded-wins-integrated-grand-prix
-and-titanium-at-cannes.

169 **"Michael Arrington started the popular technology blog *Tech-***
***Crunch*":** Liz Welch, "The Way I Work: Michael Arrington of
TechCrunch," *Inc.*, Oct. 1, 2010, www.inc.com/magazine/20101001/
the-way-i-work-michael-arrington-techcrunch.html.

170 **"*Time* magazine called it the most viral":** http://en.wikipedia.org/
wiki/Kony_2012 and http://en.wikipedia.org/wiki/Invisible_Children,
_Inc.

171 **"100,000 people in sixty countries downloaded his manifesto":** A
Brief Guide to World Domination, http://chrisguillebeau.com/3x5/a
-brief-guide-to-world-domination/.

172 **"Rian Johnson provided a downloadable MP3 audio commen-**
tary": David Cornish, "Looper Director Makes Downloadable Commentary for In-Theater Use," *Wired UK*, Oct. 10, 2012, www.wired
.com/underwire/2012/10/looper-downloadable-commentary/.

172 **" 'The World's Best Job' at $150,000 to the best-qualified appli-**
cant": Martin Lindstrom, "The 3 Best Cheap Marketing Moves of
All Time," *Fast Company*, Nov. 30, 2011, www.fastcompany.com/
node/1797997/print.

172 **"A thirty-four-year-old British charity worker named Ben Southall":**
Toni O'Loughlin, "Briton Lands 'World's Best Job' as Caretaker of
Australian Island," *The Guardian*, May 6, 2009, www.theguardian
.com/uk/2009/may/06/briton-wins-best-job-australia.

173 **"In 2011, Canon partnered with filmmaker Ron Howard":** Project
Imagin8ion Submissions, www.usa.canon.com/cusa/about_canon/
newsroom?pageKeyCode=pressreldetail&docId=0901e02480
553165.

173 **"Ron selected eight winning photos that would inspire a screen-**
play": Project Imagin8ion, http://canon.thismoment.com/.

174 **"Wieden+Kennedy created promotional kits":** Susana Polo, "We
Open a Mysterious Box, or, Paranorman Sent Us a Zombie," Aug.
1, 2012, www.themarysue.com/the-mary-sue-paranorman-zombie
-box/#0.

176 **"Christian Rudder, cofounder of the dating site OkCupid":** Jason
Del Ray, "In Love with Numbers," *Inc.*, Oct. 2010, 105.

177 **"Jerry Falwell started a church in his hometown":** Jerry Falwell,
Building Dynamic Faith (Thomas Nelson, 2007).

178 **"When Ben Silbermann launched the photo-sharing site Pinter-**

est": Paul Graham, "Do Things That Don't Scale," July 2013, http://paulgraham.com/ds.html.

179 "Chris Anderson's book *Free* tells us": Chris Anderson, *Free: The Future of a Radical Price* (Hyperion, 2009).

180 "consumers were willing to pay an average of $177": Heidi Grant Halvorson, "The Presentation Mistake You Don't Know You're Making," *Harvard Business Review*, Oct. 23, 2012, http://blogs.hbr.org/cs/2012/10/the_presentation_mistake_you_d.html.

181 "In the book *U2 by U2*, Bono recounted their experience": Neil McCormick, *U2 by U2* (It Books, 2009).

182 "Seth Godin explains in *The Dip* that people don't have a lot of time": Seth Godin, *The Dip: A Little Book That Teaches You When to Quit (and When to Stick)* (Portfolio, 2007).

CHAPTER 10

186 "Carolyn recovered the rights to her backlisted titles": Alan Rinzier, "Is There Gold in Your Backlist? Self-publish and Find Out!" *Forbes*, May 18, 2011, www.forbes.com/sites/booked/2011/05/18/is-there-gold-in-your-backlist-self-publish-and-find-out/.

188 "So she closed the studio as she knew it": Sarah Bray, "Fame and Influence: Is That What I Really Want?" Oct. 17, 2012, www.sarahjbray.com/2012/10/fame-and-influence-is-that-what-i-really-want/.

190 "Reed changed the model once again": Michael V. Copeland, "Reed Hastings: Leader of the Pack," *Fortune*, Nov. 18, 2010, http://tech.fortune.cnn.com/2010/11/18/reed-hastings-leader-of-the-pack/.

190 "Reed decided to make television shows, not films": "Once Film-Focused, Netflix Transitions to TV Shows," *The New York Times*, Feb. 27, 2012, www.nytimes.com/2012/02/28/business/media/once-film-focused-netflix-shifts-to-tv-shows.html.

190 "It's helped the company reach more than 40 million subscribers": Richard Lawler, "Netflix Tops 40 Million Customers Total, More Paid US Subscribers Than HBO," *Engadget*, Oct. 21, 2013, www.engadget.com/2013/10/21/netflix-q3-40-million-total/.

190 "Each of them cost up to $100 million to make": Felix Salmon, "Why Netflix Is Producing Original Content," Reuters, June 13, 2013, http://blogs.reuters.com/felix-salmon/2013/06/13/why-netflix-is-producing-original-content/.

191 "The dirty little secret is that seventy-five percent of the people": Ken Auletta, "You've Got News," *The New Yorker*, Jan. 24, 2011, www.newyorker.com/reporting/2011/01/24/110124fa_fact_au-letta.

192 "the company quietly tested home delivery": Bruce Horovitz, "Burger King Tries Home Delivery," *USA Today*, Jan. 16, 2012, http://usatoday30.usatoday.com/money/industries/food/story/2012-01-12/burger-king-delivery/52604104/1.

193 "The experiment was so successful that Burger King has expanded the service": "Burger King Expands Its Delivery Service to Tucson," http://finance.yahoo.com/news/burger-king-expands-delivery-tucson-130200874.html.

193 "Chipotle has grown to 1,500 stores in forty-three states": http://en.wikipedia.org/wiki/Chipotle_Mexican_Grill.

194 "ShopHouse offers bowls of beef, pork, chicken, or tofu": Bruce Horovitz, "Chipotle Founder Tries New Asian Format with Shop-House," *USA Today*, Sept. 30, 2011, http://usatoday30.usatoday.com/money/industries/food/story/2011-09-29/chipotle-shophouse-southeast-asian-kitchen/50609904/1.

194 "Chipotle announced that it was expanding the formula": Jolie Lee, "Chipotle Gets into the Pizza Business," *USA Today*, Dec. 18, 2013, www.usatoday.com/story/news/nation-now/2013/12/18/chipotle-pizza-business-expands/4113389/.

194 "Twenty-three thousand students finished the course": Andy Kessler, "Sebastian Thrun: What's Next for Silicon Valley?" *The Wall Street Journal*, June 15, 2012, http://online.wsj.com/news/articles/SB10001424052702303807404577434891291657730.

CHAPTER 11

198 "In Seth Godin's book *The Dip*, he describes how ultramarathoner Dick Collins": Seth Godin, *The Dip: A Little Book That Teaches You When to Quit (and When to Stick)* (Portfolio, 2007).

200 "Writing's still the most difficult job I've ever had": John Grisham, "Boxers, Briefs and Books," *The New York Times*, Sept. 5, 2010, www.nytimes.com/2010/09/06/opinion/06Grisham.html.

201 "starting a new endeavor 'will crush your heart like nothing else'": Howard Schultz, *Onward: How Starbucks Fought for Its Life Without Losing Its Soul* (Rodale Books, 2011).

203 " 'But if you can see that there is an arc,' he added, 'and your work belongs' ": Seth Godin, www.goodlifeproject.com/seth-godin/.

203 "Listen to what radio host Ira Glass had to say": Ira Glass, www.goodreads.com/quotes/309485-nobody-tells-this-to-people-who-are-beginners-i-wish.

203 "On November 6, 2012, the Grammy Award–winning band the Civil Wars": https://www.facebook.com/thecivilwars/posts/1015133 9645734175.

205 "they shifted the business to a flash-sale Web site": Liz Welch, "The Way I Work: Jason Goldberg, Fab.com," *Inc.*, Sept. 25, 2012, www.inc.com/magazine/201210/liz-welch/the-way-i-work-jason-goldberg-fabcom_pagen_2.html.

205 "They reached 1 million users faster than Twitter": Sarah Perez, "Fab Looks Back at Past 18 Months: 10 Million Members, 4.3 Million Products Sold," *TechCrunch*, Dec. 31, 2012, http://techcrunch.com/2012/12/31/fab-looks-back-at-past-18-months-10-million-members-4-3-million-products-sold/.

206 "he never would have taken the risks to start the company": Eric Schurenberg, "How I Did It: John Bogle of the Vanguard Group," *Inc.*, Sept. 25, 2012, www.inc.com/magazine/201210/eric-schurenberg/how-i-did-it-john-bogle-the-vanguard-group.html.

208 "That movie was *Inception*, which won four Academy Awards": http://en.wikipedia.org/wiki/Inception.

208 "the paperback version spent thirty weeks on the *New York Times* bestseller list": http://en.wikipedia.org/wiki/The_Pillars_of_the_Earth.

208 "It continues to sell more than 100,000 copies a year": http://ken-follett.com/bibliography/the_pillars_of_the_earth/.

208 "Abraham Lincoln's Career of Not Quitting": "Lincoln Never Quits," www.rogerknapp.com/inspire/lincoln.htm.

210 "George Lucas sold his *Stars Wars* franchise to Disney": "UPDATE: BREAKING: 'Star Wars' Returns—'Episode 7' Slated for 2015 and More Movies Planned as Disney Buys Lucasfilm," *Deadline*, Oct. 30, 2012, www.deadline.com/2012/10/disney-acquires-lucasfilm-star-wars-creator/.

210 "then played again for the Washington Wizards in 2001": http://en.wikipedia.org/wiki/Michael_Jordan.

210 "When comedian Jerry Seinfeld ended his successful TV show": "Seinfeld Calls Decision to End Show, 'All About Timing,' " *CNN*, Dec. 26, 1997, www.cnn.com/SHOWBIZ/9712/26/seinfeld/.

211 "Scott Belsky grew the number of members on his portfolio site":
Romain Dillet, "Adobe Acquired Portfolio Service Behance for More
Than $150 Million in Cash and Stock," *TechCrunch*, Dec. 21, 2012,
http://techcrunch.com/2012/12/21/adobe-acquired-portfolio
-service-behance-for-more-than-150-million-in-cash-and-stock/.

INDEX

needed to achieve dreams, 87–90,
185, 200
quitting and, 199
See also employment
World Wrestling Entertainment
(WWE), 139–140
Wozniak, Steve, 102

YouTube, 140, 151–152, 153,
169–170

Zappos, 152
Zipcar, 43, 53
Zuckerberg, Mark, 127
Zumba, 71–72